AN INTRODUCTION TO
DRAWING THE NUDE

ANATOMY · FORM · COMPOSITION · MOVEMENT · STRUCTURE · PROPORTION

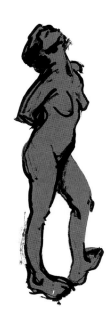

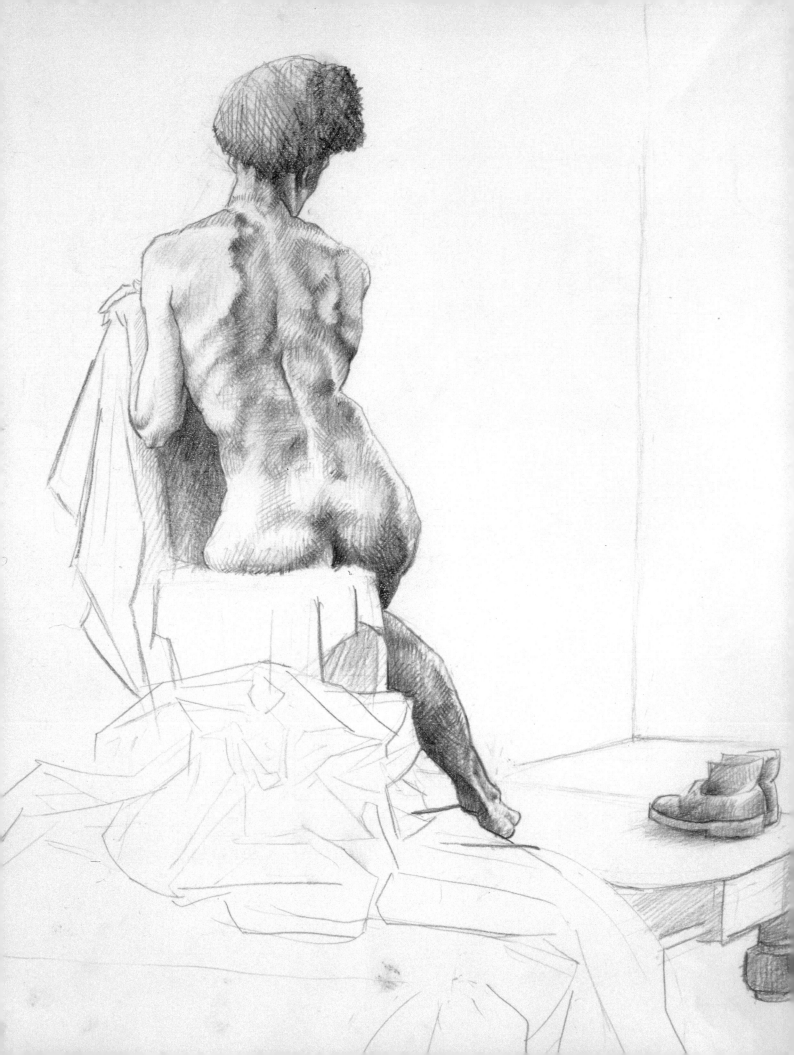

AN INTRODUCTION TO
DRAWING THE NUDE

ANATOMY · PROPORTION · BALANCE · MOVEMENT · LIGHT · COMPOSITION

DIANA CONSTANCE

CHARTWELL
BOOKS, INC.

A QUINTET BOOK

Published by Chartwell Books
A Division of Book Sales, Inc.
110 Enterprise Avenue
Secaucus, New Jersey 07094

This edition produced for sale in the U.S.A.,
its territories and dependencies only.

ISBN 1–55521–901–2

This book was designed and produced by
Quintet Publishing Limited
6 Blundell Street
London N7 9BH

Creative Director: Richard Dewing
Designer: Ian Hunt
Project Editor: Helen Denholm
Editor: Lydia Darbyshire
Photographers: Paul Forrester and Martin Norris

With thanks to Lyra (UK) Ltd and Daler Rowney
for supplying artists' materials for photography

Typeset in Great Britain by
Central Southern Typesetters, Eastbourne
Manufactured in Hong Kong by
Regent Publishing Services Limited
Printed in Singapore by Star Standard Industries Pte. Ltd.

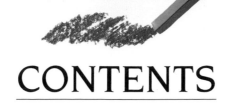

CONTENTS

INTRODUCTION

The nude has been one of the more changeable images in art. The depiction of the human image has seldom been objective. It has always been a reflection of the cultural and religious attitudes of its time. As the human image now begins to re-emerge after years of non-figurative art, the need arises to rediscover the knowledge of anatomy and the skills of drawing and to put them in a modern context so that we can leave a legacy of our own image.

The ancient Greeks saw the nude as the sum of human beauty and endeavor, as reflected in the *Belvedere Apollo*. However, with the passing of the pagan world, there began the Christian concept of man, son of Adam, who was conceived and born in sin, This was reflected in the artistic representation of the human figure by a new degree of shame and self-consciousness.

The climb out of that abyss of self-abasement began with the rediscovery of the Greco-Roman literature and art which signaled the Renaissance. The nude once again became the touchstone of art, one example being Botticelli's *Venus*, exulting in her own beauty. Tragically, the reaction to this new liberalism was fear and religious fanaticism, and many artists, including Botticelli (1445–1510), threw their own work into the bonfire of the vanities in Florence in 1497. The topmost tiers of the pyre were reserved for paintings and drawings of beautiful women.

The repression, however, was short-lived, and the cultured Venetians were willing patrons for the young Titian whose images of voluptuous nudes were enthusiastically copied in the courts north of the Alps, where the semi-pagan allegories of Rubens (1557–1640) reflected the fruits of earthly power. Today we perhaps identify more with the ordinary women of Rembrandt's canvases.

In France, for about a century and a half, the nude became the frivolous plaything of the French aristocracy, only to emerge after the Revolution in the new image of *La Madelaine*, with the sturdy republican virtues of David (1748–1825). Then, with the collapse of the hopes and ideals of the republic and the empire, the female nude became a hapless victim of romantic fantasy in the historical paintings of Delacroix and his contemporaries. With a curious piquancy, one of the minor figures in *The Crusaders Entering Constantinople*, by Delacroix (1798–1863), was transformed into the primary inspiration for Degas's (1834–1917) series of paintings of women at their toilettes.

The portrayal of the nude in Manet's *Déjeuner sur l'herbe* scandalized society. This stir had less to do with the figure itself than with the context in which she was seen – sharing a picnic with a group of fully clothed painters.

The last decade of the 19th century saw in the creations of Degas, Gauguin, Toulouse-Lautrec, and Rodin some of the finest works of art to have been inspired by the nude. As we reach the end of the 20th century, interest in figurative art is returning, and with it comes the need to study the nude.

This book is intended for both art students and amateurs. The discipline of drawing the figure develops from a study of anatomy, proportion, balance, and movement. It continues with the expression of space and light, which are the tools that artists use to create the illusion of reality and life on a two-dimensional surface, but in the end it is the drawing of a human being

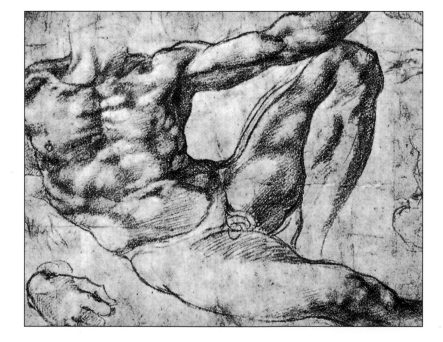

L E F T **A study of Adam's torso made by Michelangelo (1475–1564) in preparation for his work on the Sistine Chapel.**

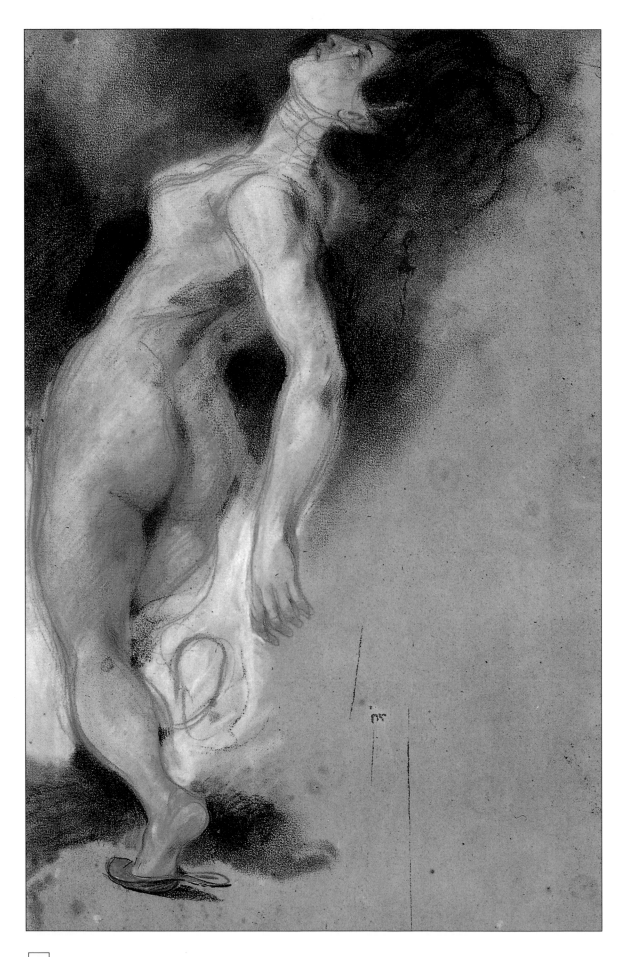

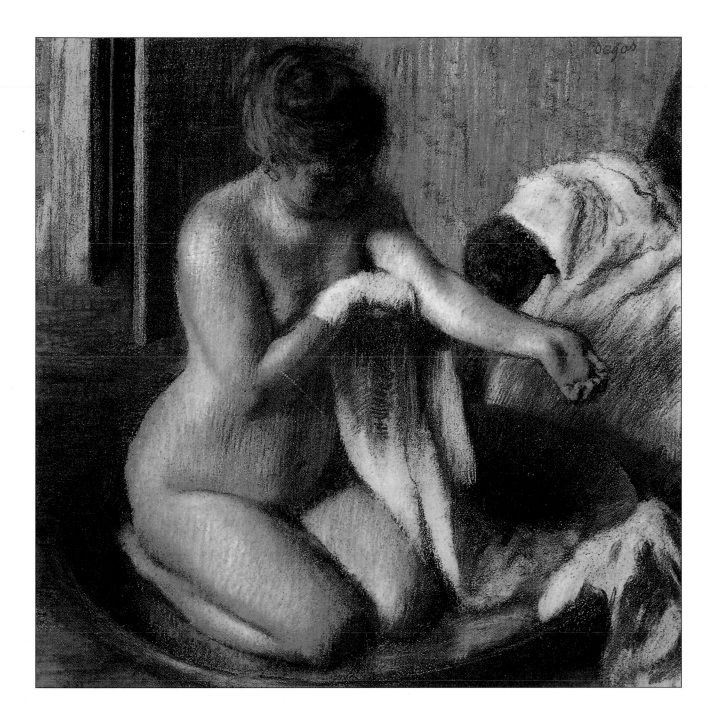

ABOVE *Woman in a Tub* by Edgar Degas (1834–1917), a soft pastel study on buff-colored paper.

OPPOSITE *Slave girl*, study for *The Death of Sardanapalus* by Eugène Delacroix (1798–1863) in pastel on buff-colored paper.

that is the artist's first consideration.

Unfortunately, the model in a life class can easily become a part of the furnishings. I believe that if a choice must be made between an immediate and spontaneous impression of the person and accuracy, it is best to follow your feelings, for it is the spirit that informs.

I am grateful to the many students, postgraduate students, and contemporary artists whose work is illustrated on these pages.

This new generation of artists will ensure that the figure will emerge once again as a major source of inspiration. "The greatest art always returns to the vulnerability of the human situation" (Francis Bacon, b. 1909).

1
MATERIALS AND EQUIPMENT

Understanding the potential and deficiencies of the different drawing materials is a vital first step in our studies. Not all papers are suitable for dry stick media, such as charcoal, conte pencil, or pastel. These media require paper with a slight tooth or roughness because they tend to slide over the surface of a smooth paper. The quality and price of paper vary enormously, ranging from those made of wood pulp, which still contain acid, to fine, handmade watercolor paper, which is 100 percent cotton and acid-free. It is important to find an inexpensive paper for learning and taking risks with. so that you feel free to do as many drawings as possible. However, when you are doing more finished drawings, you will want a paper that will not turn brown or crumble in six months.

DRAWING MEDIA

Pencils

Artists' pencils are graded from H (hard) to B (soft). A 2H pencil will give you a very sharp, light line, while an 8B will give a heavier, darker line. When you choose a medium, try to match the appropriate size and weight of line to the right size of paper. Pencil is suitable for sketchbook drawing and medium-sized sketch pads. The line is, however, too light and thin to sustain a strong image on a large format. There are, of course, exceptions to this rule: you can use a soft pencil to crosshatch; if you apply strong pressure, you can build up very satisfactory dark shading over a large area.

Graphite sticks

These sticks are made of the same material that forms the "lead" of a pencil – graphite. It is produced in stick form so that you can work either with the side, to produce a gray pencil tone, or with the point, when it is like a soft, wide pencil. Graphite sticks can be sharpened with a mat knife to form a wedge-shaped point, which will enable you to go from a thin line to a broad line simply by turning the stick slightly.

Drawings done with a graphite stick do not have to be sprayed with a fixative. Erase any errors with a kneaded eraser, a plastic eraser, or fresh bread.

Colored pencils

There are several different types of colored pencils available, and they vary in brilliance and softness. Try them out before you buy, because they are quite expensive and fragile. Take care not to drop them, as the lead inside will shatter.

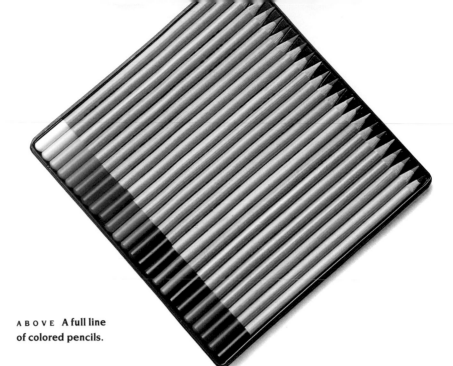

ABOVE **A full line of colored pencils.**

Colored pencils are suitable for small drawings, and they can be erased with a kneaded eraser or a plastic eraser.

Charcoal

Avoid using any type of charcoal on smooth papers, such as newsprint, because the stick slides over the surface too quickly, giving an insipid line. I advise my students to use lining paper and to cut it to the length they need for quick, disposable sketches. For better drawings, use drawing or sketch pads, or charcoal paper.

Willow pencils are ideal for quick sketches. Compressed charcoal sticks are available in different grades; they are heavier and darker than charcoal pencils and can give you a rich, dark tone quickly. A good drawing with charcoal sticks can resemble a lithograph.

All charcoal can be erased with a kneaded eraser or fresh bread. I would always use bread first with charcoal sticks to avoid "rubbing in" the heavy charcoal. With bread you can gently lift it off without damaging the surface of the paper. Completed drawings should be sprayed with fixative. To avoid smudging a drawing, keep it covered with an overlay of thin tracing paper. I prefer tracing paper, which remains flat, to tissue paper, which crumples easily.

BELOW **From left to right: willow charcoal; pencils; Chinese brush; small flat sable brush; bamboo pen; Chinese brush; large sable brush; pastel pencil in shades.**

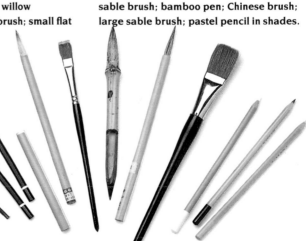

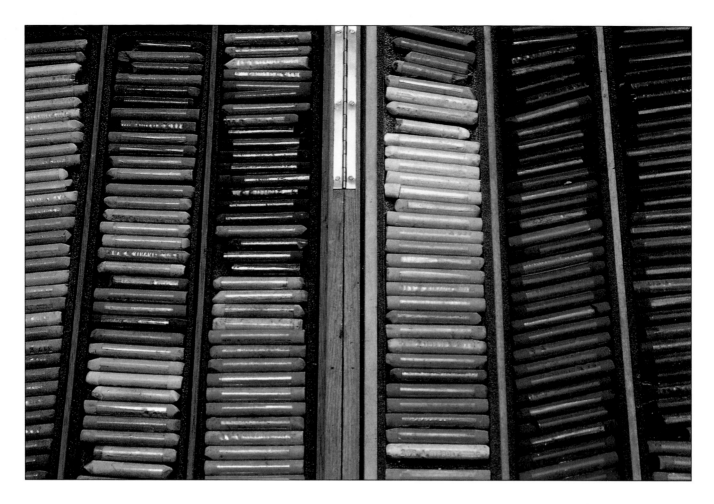

Conte crayons

These are rather hard sticks of pigment, bound with gum arabic. They can be sharpened with a sandpaper block and used on the point or on the side. Alternatively, they can be broken to make a sharp edge. The original colors used by the Renaissance masters were sienna, umber, and black. White conte or softer white pastel can be used for highlighting. A lightly textured paper is the best support, but heavier grades of paper can also be used.

Erase conte crayon with a kneaded eraser or fresh bread.

Pastels

There are three types of pastel. Soft pastel, which has been used for most of the pastel work in this book, is a round stick, and, as its name suggests, is very soft and easily blended or layered.

Neopastel (or Nupastel) is a square-edged, thin stick. It is much harder than soft pastel, and

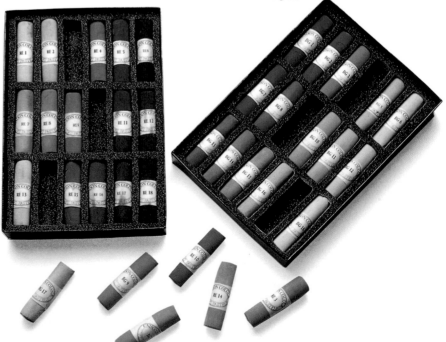

ABOVE **A full line of soft French pastels, conveniently boxed.**

BELOW **Unison pastels: large sticks of pastel developed in the north of England capture the subtle colors and light of the local landscapes.**

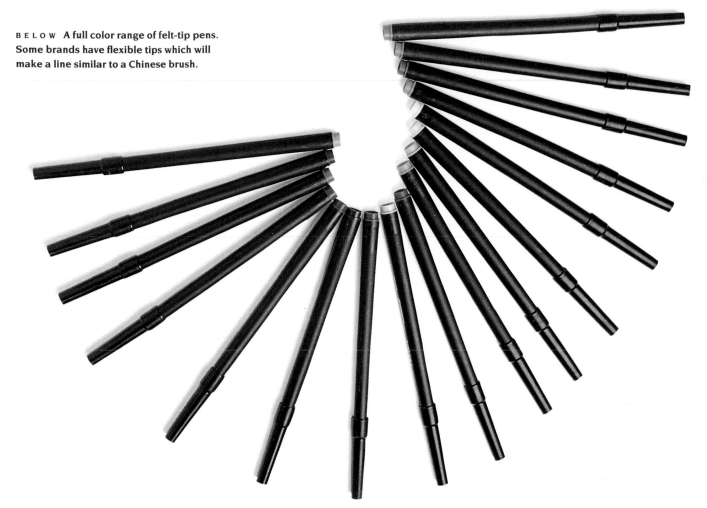

although it can be blended, the hardness makes layering very difficult. It can be used to make a sharp line or for small-scale work.

Oil pastel, which is based on an oil and wax binder, is totally different from the other kinds of pastel, which are bonded together with water and gum.

Felt-tip pens

The introduction of felt-tip pens revolutionized pen and ink drawing and gave us a marvelously adaptable, fluid line to work with. Beware, however, of pens with fugitive inks – your drawings will begin to fade in a year. Permanent colors, although in a limited choice, are available, and new ones are being developed so that we should soon have a full range of permanent colors from which to choose. Some felt-tip pens have flexible tips, which give a fluid, attractive brush line.

Felt-tip pen cannot be erased.

Bamboo pens and reeds

These pens have been used for centuries. They give a very varied line and work best on a small scale with India ink on watercolor paper. They do take time to get used to, and the tips have to be lightly scraped before use to remove any accumulation of dry ink.

Brushes

The finest brushes you can buy are made of sable, and unfortunately they are very expensive. They will, however, last for many years, retaining their natural spring if you take good care of them. Wash your brushes in lukewarm water immediately after use, and if you have used India ink, wash them using mild hand soap. Shake excess water out of the brushes and allow them to dry, standing them in a glass or jar with the bristles up so that the fine sable hairs are straight. Never use a sable brush with acrylic paint. When you buy a sable brush, check how well it points and springs back by dipping it in clear water and using it on a piece of paper. A good supplier of artists' materials will always have a jar of water for this purpose near the brushes.

Squirrel brushes are cheaper and can be used for rough work, but they are not such good quality as sable and they tend to resemble a mop more than a brush. There are good lines of nylon brushes for use with acrylics, and Chinese brushes, available from art supply stores, can be used for brush and wash drawings.

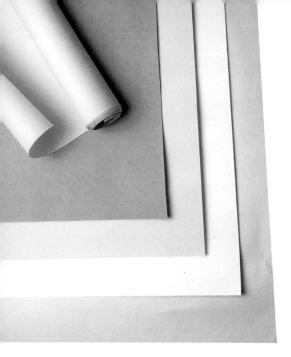

PAPER

Newsprint

Although newsprint paper is widely used, I consider it a poor choice for most work. It is usually too smooth for use with charcoal or conte, although you may be fortunate and find some that has a flat surface which will be perfectly adequate for quick drawings. However, because it is made from wood pulp, which contains acid, the life of newsprint is short – expect it to turn brown and crumble after a few years.

Lining paper

Lining paper is a good, inexpensive

BELOW The quality of a line changes as different media move across different surfaces of paper. Note the strong texture in the white watercolor paper.

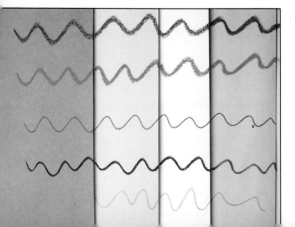

paper and can be bought from any hardware store. Cut it to the length you need and flatten it under a weight, such as a pile of books. It has an adequate surface to hold charcoal or conte. It is not permanent, as the acid content will cause it to brown in a year or two.

Brown wrapping paper

The flat side of brown wrapping paper provides an interesting surface and tone. It is inexpensive and comes in large sheets. However, it is not permanent and will become brittle after a few years.

Construction paper

Construction paper has a rough texture, but, like newsprint, it is not permanent and the surface can easily be damaged by erasing.

Bond paper

Bond paper is the standard drawing paper. It is widely available and has a good life expectancy.

Charcoal paper

Charcoal is heavier than bond paper. It has a light texture, which is suitable for charcoal, conte, and pastels, and it can absorb a wash fairly well. Like cartridge, it is reasonably permanent.

Ingres paper

Ingres is a lightweight, good quality paper with a fine textural pattern. Although it is suitable for charcoal, conte, and pastels, it is too light for washes. It is permanent.

Pastel paper

Pastel paper is available in different shades and colors, although I try to avoid the strong colors. It is ideal for a quick pastel study. Conte crayon with chalk for highlighting can also

be used to good effect on this paper, but it is not suitable for washes. It is reasonably permanent.

Watercolor paper

Watercolor paper comes in weights ranging from 70lb (150g) to 400lb (850g). For the average drawing 90lb (185g) should be adequate. Watercolor paper varies considerably in texture and can be used with all media, including pen and ink and wash. The best paper is 100 percent cotton and acid-free. Using a pure cotton paper is important for watercolor if the colors are to stay bright and true, but it does not make much difference to pastel and charcoal. However, the toughness and the strong texture are very important if you want to build up many layers of pastel. Make sure that any paper you use is acid-free for permanence and to avoid browning.

Watercolor paper can be prepared by giving it a wash of color or tone and stretched so that it doesn't buckle when watercolor is applied. Watercolor, gouache, or acrylic can be used for the wash.

PRESERVING AND STORING DRAWINGS

Ideally, artist's fixative should be used on all charcoal, conte, and pastel drawings. Hair spray, which is cheaper, is often used, but it fixes the drawing poorly and may cause discoloration in time. A better, inexpensive alternative is liquid fixative, which you can blow on with a small diffuser. Both can be purchased from art supply stores. Charcoal, conte, and pastel drawings should also be covered with an overlay of tracing or tissue paper to protect them as they are being moved or stored.

2

ANATOMY

The study of the skeleton is the core of all life drawing. This great armature holds the key to the movements of the body, and although you do not need to know the names of all the 200 or so bones, it is important to know how they relate to each other. It is also necessary to appreciate the size of the joints and the ways in which they work.

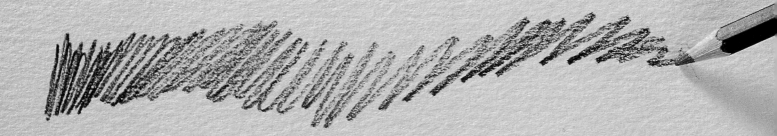

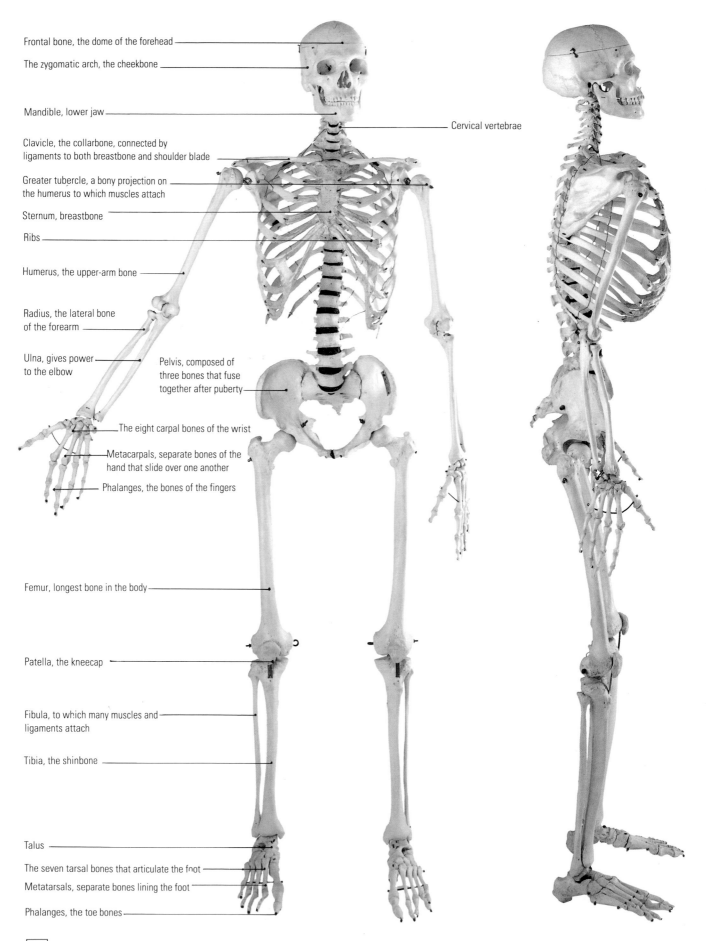

Frontal bone, the dome of the forehead

The zygomatic arch, the cheekbone

Mandible, lower jaw

Clavicle, the collarbone, connected by
ligaments to both breastbone and shoulder blade

Greater tubercle, a bony projection on
the humerus to which muscles attach

Sternum, breastbone

Ribs

Humerus, the upper-arm bone

Radius, the lateral bone
of the forearm

Ulna, gives power
to the elbow

Cervical vertebrae

Pelvis, composed of
three bones that fuse
together after puberty

The eight carpal bones of the wrist

Metacarpals, separate bones of the
hand that slide over one another

Phalanges, the bones of the fingers

Femur, longest bone in the body

Patella, the kneecap

Fibula, to which many muscles and
ligaments attach

Tibia, the shinbone

Talus

The seven tarsal bones that articulate the foot

Metatarsals, separate bones lining the foot

Phalanges, the toe bones

THE SKELETON

When you examine a human skeleton for the first time, you may be surprised by the degree of curvature in the spine as it describes a double S-bend, from the base of the skull through to the vestigial tail, the coccyx. When you are drawing, remember how easily the spine twists and bends in its long, curving rhythm. Most people draw the curve of the back correctly, but forget the curve in the vertebrae of the neck, which makes the head jut forward.

The arms are connected to, and suspended from, the collarbones and shoulder blades. These bones are attached to the main frame of the body by tendons and muscles instead of joints. A diamond-shaped muscle, the trapezius, fans across the back from the vertebrae to the shoulder joint. It wraps over the shoulder blades, which, thus secured, can safely slide over the back plane, giving the shoulders a wide variety of movements.

The upper arm with its single bone, the humerus, is quite straight-forward, but the lower arm is one of the most difficult parts of the body to draw correctly. The bones are called the ulna and radius. The latter moves across the ulna as you make a circular movement of your hand. Turn your palm up and look at your lower arm. If you turn your palm to the floor, you will see the radius cross over the ulna. The movement of the bones profoundly affects the shape of the lower arm.

When we look at our hands, the mass of muscle and tendon hides the fact that the finger bones, the phalanges, are extensions of the metacarpals (the bones extending

OPPOSITE **A front and side view of the full skeleton. The side view shows the S-bend of the spine.**

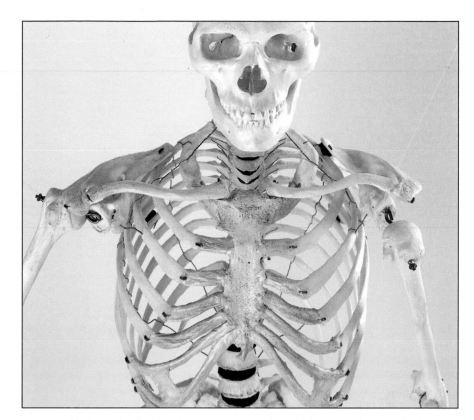

ABOVE **Skeleton showing how the collarbones and shoulder bones girdle the top of the rib cage. The clavicle, at the base** of the neck between the two collarbones, is the balance point of the body.

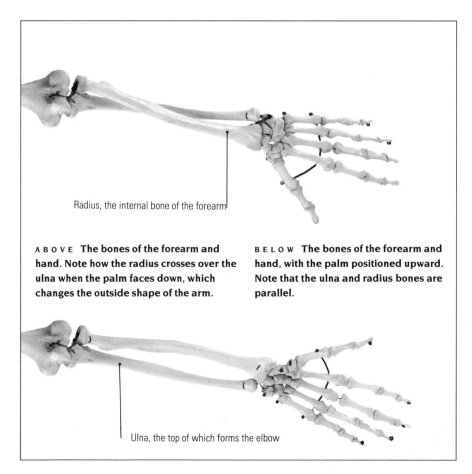

Radius, the internal bone of the forearm

ABOVE **The bones of the forearm and hand. Note how the radius crosses over the ulna when the palm faces down, which changes the outside shape of the arm.**

BELOW **The bones of the forearm and hand, with the palm positioned upward. Note that the ulna and radius bones are parallel.**

Ulna, the top of which forms the elbow

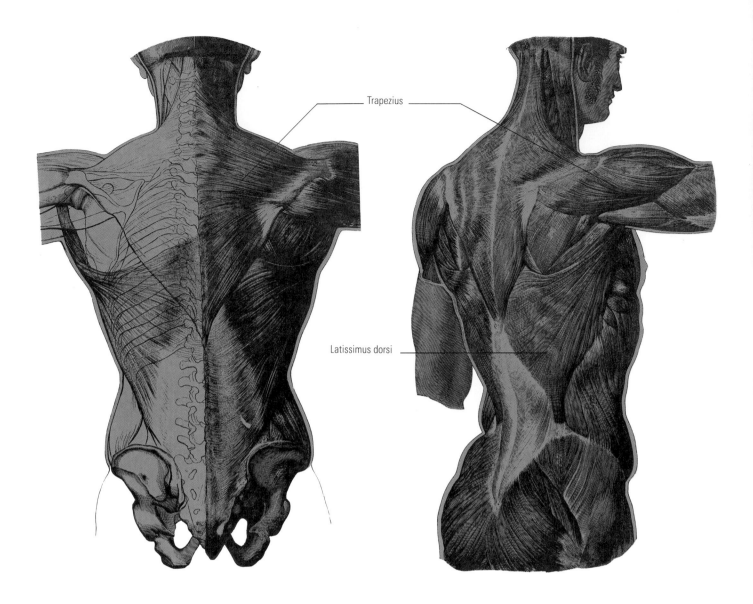

Trapezius

Latissimus dorsi

from the wrist to the base of the fingers), which are similar in shape. When you draw a hand, notice how the movement starts and comes down from the wrist through to the fingers. It is a mistake to think of the body of the hand as a stiff block with the movement confined to the fingers.

The rib cage is shaped like an inverted basket. It radiates out from the spine, to wrap around and protect our vital organs, and projects outward to a depth greater than that of the head. The pelvis, which is attached to the base of the spine, resembles a saddle. There is a gap of approximately one head's

length between the last rib and the pelvis, with only the flexible spine connecting the two.

When you look at the skeleton of the abdomen without its covering of muscles, you can appreciate the tremendous range of bending and twisting movements that can be made. If we underestimate this space and the flexibility it gives, our drawings will look stiff and squashed.

The greater trochanter of the femur, the hipbone, projects beyond the edge of the pelvis. The hip joint is a ball-and-socket joint, which permits a variety of movements. The knees are not thin

ABOVE LEFT **The trapezius is a diamond-shaped sheet of muscle that connects the shoulders to the spinal vertebrae.**

ABOVE RIGHT **The latissimus dorsi wraps around the sides of the trunk and connects under the pectoral muscles of the chest, where it twists as it joins the bicipital groove of the humerus. This muscle helps us to swing the upper part of our torso.**

OPPOSITE LEFT **The pectorialis major, the chest muscle, is attached to the sternum. It stretches over the top of the ribs, turning and tucking under where it joins the humerus. This twist creates the thick fold leading into the armpit. The rectus abdominus is the long crease that runs down from the clavicle along the breastbone, between the abdominal muscles to the genitals. Look for this line when trying to see movement and direction.**

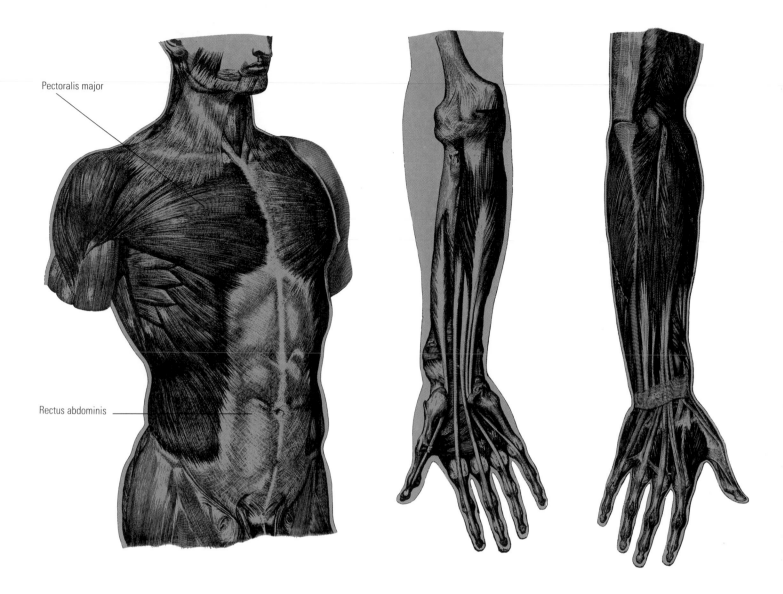

Pectoralis major

Rectus abdominis

and delicate; they are massive, measuring approximately half the width of the skull. They work like a hinge, with a more restricted movement than the hip joint.

The ankle, another type of hinge, allows a limited sideways movement. The bulge on the inside of the ankle, the bottom of the tibia bone, is higher than the bone on the outside, the bottom of the fibula bone, and both bones straddle the top of the foot. The calcaneus, the heel bone, extends well behind the ankle. It is quite easy to see in the skeleton the way in which the foot arches on the inside and slopes sideways, giving a flat profile on the

outside. Careful drawings of the skeleton are very important.

MUSCLES AND TENDONS

There are over 400 muscles in the body, but mercifully artists need only concern themselves with the major ones of movement. Tendons are the connective tissues between bone and muscle. The contraction or extension of the muscle has the effect of a pulley on the bone to which it is connected, and this simple action, coordinated and multiplied many times over, enables us to move in hundreds of ways or to stand reasonably still.

Muscles vary in shape. The most

ABOVE MIDDLE The inner part of the forearm is flat, but this shape changes as the arm is turned. As the outside of the forearm and wrist come around and over the inner arm, the diagonal line of the radius may be seen crossing over.

ABOVE RIGHT The back view of the forearm and hand. The profiles of the two sides of the arm are quite different. The muscles of the outer side of the arm are connected higher than those on the inner side. The muscles end in long tendons, which connect to the wrists.

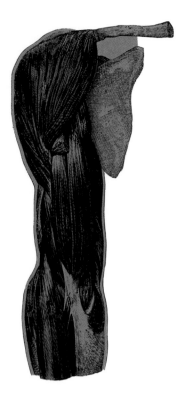

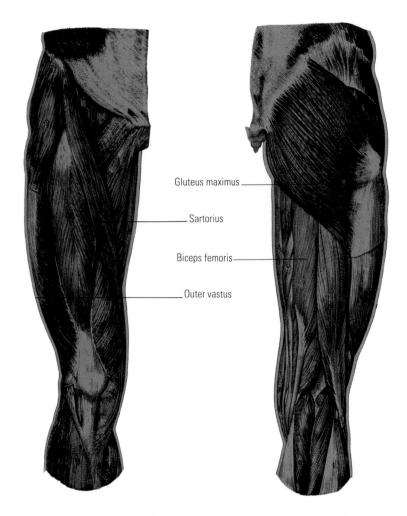

Gluteus maximus

Sartorius

Biceps femoris

Outer vastus

ABOVE **The deltoid muscles that form the shoulder cap raise and lower the arm. The triceps on the back of the upper arm pull the lower arm straight or downward, while the biceps at the front raise the lower arm.**

ABOVE **The outer vastus curves down from the head of the femur to the knee. It is followed by a strap-like muscle called the sartorius, which runs diagonally down from the hip and crosses over the thigh to join the inside of the knee. The result is a graceful, twisting line.**

ABOVE **The gluteus maximus runs diagonally from the back to join the flat ilio tibial band on the side of the thigh.**

common type of long muscle found in the body is the fusiform, which resembles a spindle. It may be clearly seen in the biceps of the upper arm and the gastrocnemius or calf muscle. As you may know, when you have to pull something heavy, it helps to shorten the tow rope. The same principle is found in the body, where several short muscles are joined together along a long shaft of tendon to give additional strength. These flat muscles are called the penniforms and bipenniforms because they resemble one- or two-sided feathers.

They are enormously strong, stretching across the back, chest, and abdomen.

The different shapes of the muscles will produce either rounded surfaces or flat planes in the body. For this reason it is wise to copy illustrations of the muscles so that you can differentiate among the complex and hidden forms under layers of skin and tissue.

The muscles we use for movement are known as voluntary muscles because we are able to control them consciously. However, many muscles in the body are not

controlled by a conscious decision. These are the involuntary muscles, which are controlled automatically, from the back of the brain. The involuntary muscles include the diaphragm, which helps us to breathe; the muscles of the heart, which contract and pump blood around our bodies; and the muscles of the alimentary canal, which push food through the digestive system. The effects of the involuntary muscles become visible and concern the artist only when they begin to malfunction – the blue tinge of the lips when the heart is failing, and

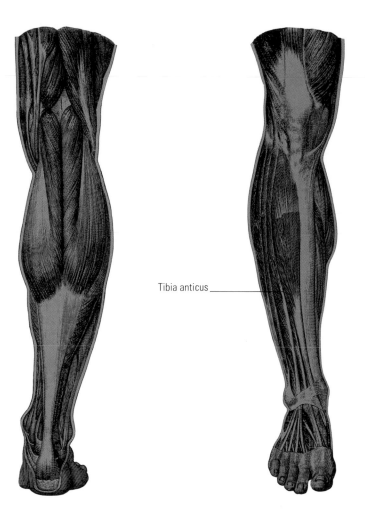

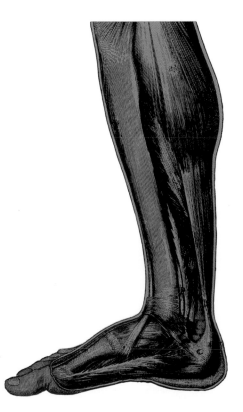

Tibia anticus

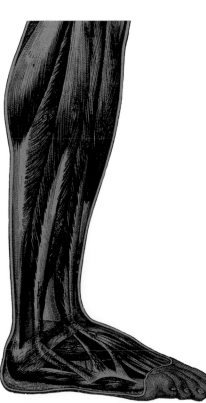

the distortions of the belly when the muscles of the alimentary canal falter.

Men and women have the same basic muscles, but the development of their structure and the extra tissue which is stored nutrient for a pregnant or nursing woman, make the woman's figure distinctively different. The widest part of a man's body is usually across his shoulders; a woman's hips are usually either wider than or the same as her shoulders.

After studying the body's basic structure, we have to take into consideration the modifications that occur at different periods of our lives. The plump roundness of infancy changes to the lean angles of early youth, while in time the clearly defined muscles of a young person will be partially obscured by the increased thickness of the fat layers. The gradual stretching and loosening of the muscles as a person ages change the profile of the body. As the back muscles give way, for example, the shoulders become rounder and the chest compresses.

3

PROPORTION

Proportions are as variable as people. Drawing from the nude quickly makes you aware that the differences between people only start with their faces — their real individuality is the whole body; the ideal or standard figure is seldom seen. Real people are much more interesting.

Artists measure the proportions of the human figure in terms of a person's head. Some people are six heads high; others are nine heads high. The proportions of their legs and torsos differ as well. Although it is useful for beginners to know the proportions of the average person, this should be only a temporary guide to be used until you have developed the skill to see and draw the individual.

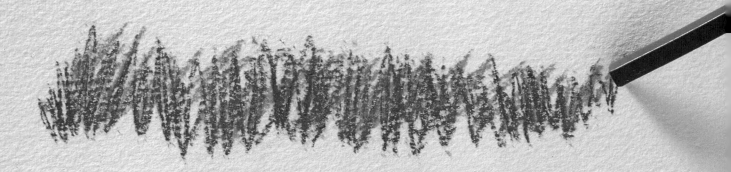

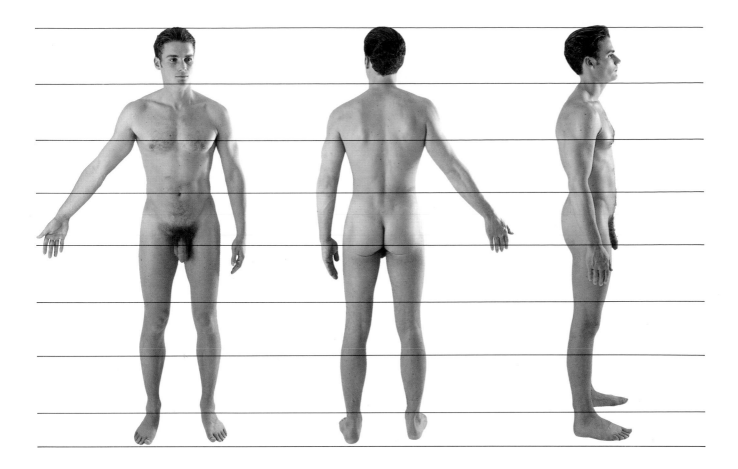

THE STANDARD FIGURE

The average person is approximately seven and a half heads tall. The bodies of men and women have evolved to suit their biological destiny, and it is possible to tell whether the skeleton that usually hangs in a life class was a man's or a woman's by looking at the shape of the pelvis. A woman's pelvis is wider at the top, deeper, and capacious enough to support the fetus. The distance from her waist to her crotch is longer. No amount of dieting will ever give a woman the slim hips of a man. A man's shoulders are wider than a woman's and his legs longer, as befits his original role as hunter/gatherer. The softer curves and rounded shapes of a woman's figure are nature's way of providing extra stored energy and insulation for mother and child in the form of a clothing of thin layers of fat.

When you are drawing the standing figure, the pubic area will be just below the mid-point of the body. The hands will reach the mid-point of the thighs, while the elbows are at the level of the waist. Most people draw the feet far too small. They are at least one head in length, and the hands are slightly shorter.

If you wish to draw the shape of an individual figure, measure from the clavicles or collarbones down to the pubic area and compare this to the length of the legs. Then measure across the shoulders and hips and compare their width. This will give you the model's characteristic shape and proportions.

The characteristics that mark out the individual are numerous, but looking at the extremes may enable you to place your model somewhere between the two. First, a very thin, emaciated person will look angular and appear to have joints that are too large for his or her body. The skull will seem to protrude through the head; the teeth will be prominent; the hands and feet will be oversized; the legs will seem to be bowed, although this is an illusion caused by the shrinkage of the thighs. At the other extreme, an obese person will look blown up, the enlarged abdomen preventing the arms from hanging straight down so that they stand away from the sides; wrists, hands, and feet will appear disproportionately small.

ABOVE **Front, back, and side view of a standing male. He is 7½ heads high, the middle of his body being at the pubic area. The back view shows how his shoulders are slightly wider than his hips. He stands with his weight evenly divided, the weight falling between his feet. Note how in the side view his neck does not sit on top of his shoulders, but thrusts forward from the collar bones.**

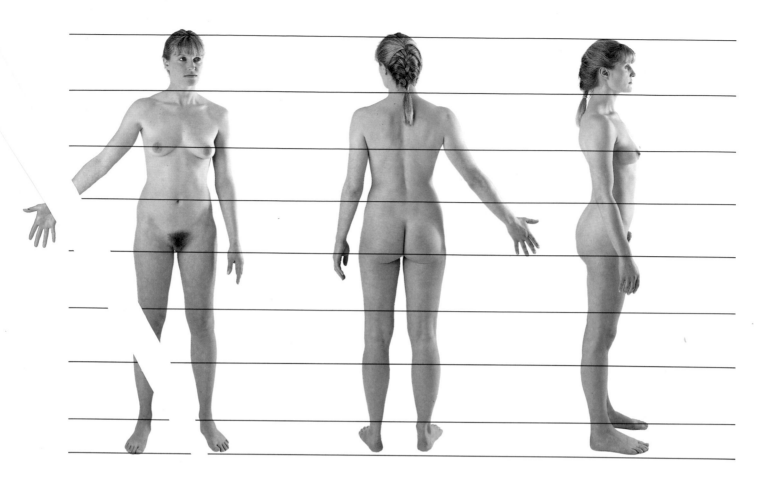

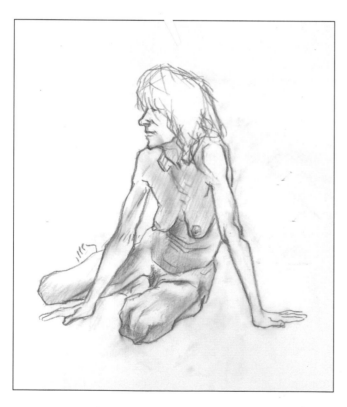

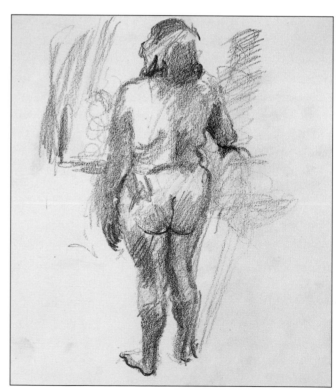

ABOVE A conte drawing using sharp lines and angles to show the emaciated quality of this woman.

RIGHT In this pencil sketch, the figure's corpulent flesh hangs loosely from the frame.

TOP Proportions of the female. She stands slightly less than 7¼ heads high, and her torso is longer than a male's. Her hips are wider than her shoulders.

THE PROPORTIONS OF THE HEAD

The bottom of the eye socket is the mid-point of the face. The ears are on a line with the eyebrow and the end of the nose. There is one eye's width between the eyes. Portrait artists measure the triangles made by the eyes and the end of the nose and by the eyes and the chin. These triangles give an accurate indication of the shape of the person's face. The skull is as deep as the length of the face, and the back of the skull is slightly wider than the face.

PROPORTIONAL CHANGES DUE TO AGING

A baby's proportions are very different from an adult's. The mid-point of the body is the navel, and the body length is four heads, three-quarters of that length being the head and abdomen, while the legs are a mere one-quarter. The cranium is disproportionately larger than the face, while the chin is small to help the baby nurse.

As a child grows, the limbs lengthen, and the jaw fills out and moves forward. At puberty the male and female adult proportions emerge. The male muscular development produces an angular, leaner look, while the first large deposits of fat give a girl the characteristic smooth curvature of her sex. The female breasts develop, and both sexes grow body hair. The shoulder bones of the male are the last bones to reach their full length, which happens in the early twenties, and until that time the youth will have a thinner, more vertical appearance.

As we age, our bodies increase in weight and mass, until we reach old age, when the shrinkage of the inter-

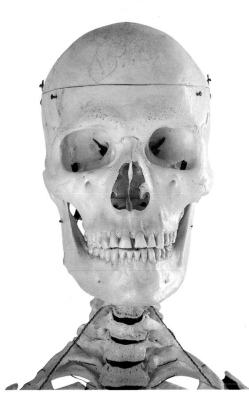

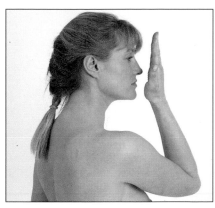

A B O V E The length of the face is approximately the same length as the hand. The depth of the skull is equal to the length of the front.

L E F T A young person's skull. The bottom of the eye sockets are about halfway down the skull, and the widest point is at the cheekbones.

vertebral disks in the spine and the bending of the head of the thigh bone under the weight of the head and torso cause us to lose up to half a head in height. Our shoulders bend forward because the spine is no longer able to support the weight. A last irony is that the cranial sutures of our skulls, which were open at birth, finally disappear.

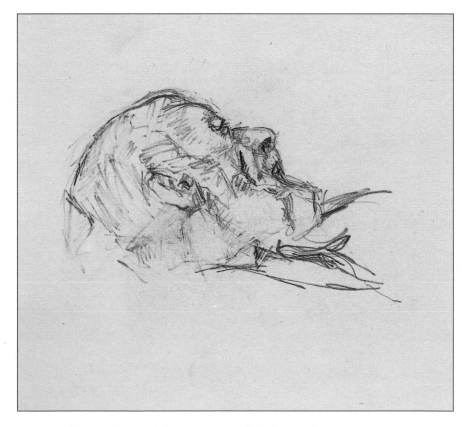

A B O V E This sensitive pencil drawing shows the effects of aging. The jaw muscles have loosened, causing the angle of the chin to recede.

4

MEASUREMENT

It is reputed that Picasso, in a bravura demonstration of his talent, drew a nude, starting with the toe and carrying on up the figure without stoppng. The thought is breathtaking to anyone familiar with the problems of life drawing, when careful observation supported by precise measurement is usually needed. Unfortunately, the untrained eye frequently misleads, so a simple observation of the model has to be checked against careful measurement.

THE CORRECT POSITION AT THE EASEL

First, if you are standing at an easel, as I hope you are, put your board and paper at the same level as your eyes. If you have a very large sheet of paper, you must move the drawing board up or down to keep the part of the drawing you are working on at your eye level. It is always best to stand at an easel so that you can step back from the drawing to see the whole image. If you must use a stool, check for distortions in the lower half of the drawing. Next, whether you are standing or sitting, place yourself where you can see both the model and your paper at the same time without having to look around the side of the drawing board or change your position in any way to see the model. In other words, do not bury yourself behind the board.

TRADITIONAL MEASUREMENT

The traditional method of measuring the proportions of the body is to hold a pencil vertically, with arm outstretched. Line up the end of the pencil with the top of the model's head and, by moving your thumb on the pencil, mark the length of the head. Keep the measurement on the pencil with your thumb so that you can compare that length to other parts of the body and measure their relationships precisely.

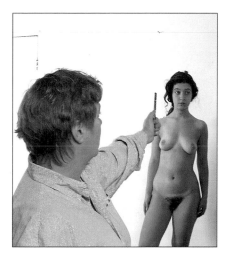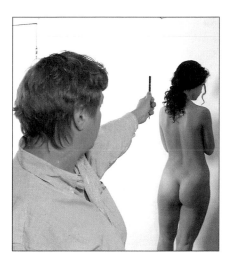

A B O V E **The artist, using the traditional method, measures the length of the head on a pencil.**

THE MOVABLE GRID

I have developed another version of the traditional measuring method, which I find useful. Holding a pencil or ruler vertically, I slowly move it across my line of vision of the model. In this way I can see not only where the balance of weight of the body is falling, but also where the different parts of the body line up underneath each other. I do the same thing again, but holding the pencil horizontally, this time moving it from head to foot in my line of vision with the figure. By moving the pencil across and then up and down in this way, you are looking through a movable grid.

When you begin, you may find it helpful to draw on graph paper, and this will be a very useful method of measurement when you come to draw the foreshortened figure.

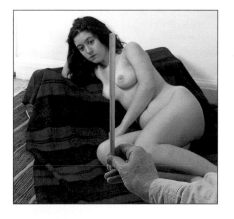

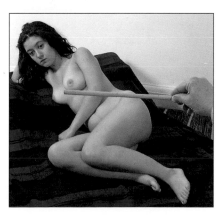

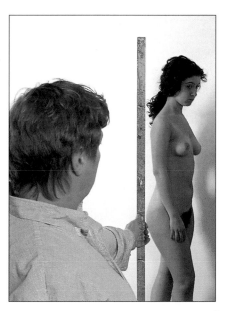

A B O V E **A ruler held vertically helps the artist appreciate the direction and profile of the body.**

A B O V E L E F T A N D L E F T **Using the movable grid, the artist holds a stick across the form vertically and horizontally to show the juxtaposition of the limbs.**

NEGATIVE SPACE

The term negative space refers to that area surrounding the figure. Drawing this negative space or marking out this area is one of the best methods of measurement that I know, and it is particularly useful when you have a foreshortened pose. By looking at the area outside the model's body, you can measure the parts of the body against the background shapes or against other parts of the figure. So, if the model has her hand on her hip, the shape of the triangle between arm and waist can tell you more about the length of the upper and lower arm than any other method of measurement.

Our observation becomes limited when we fix our gaze on the body alone, and this method of measurement gives us a means of looking at the pose with fresh eyes. You can draw negative space either as a means of checking your measurements or as a valuable exercise in better observation.

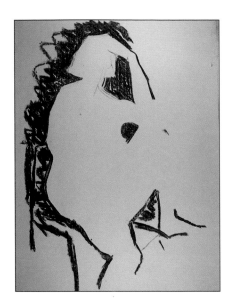

ABOVE **A charcoal drawing of the negative space. The artist is slowly working around the space outside the figure and trying to draw only that.**

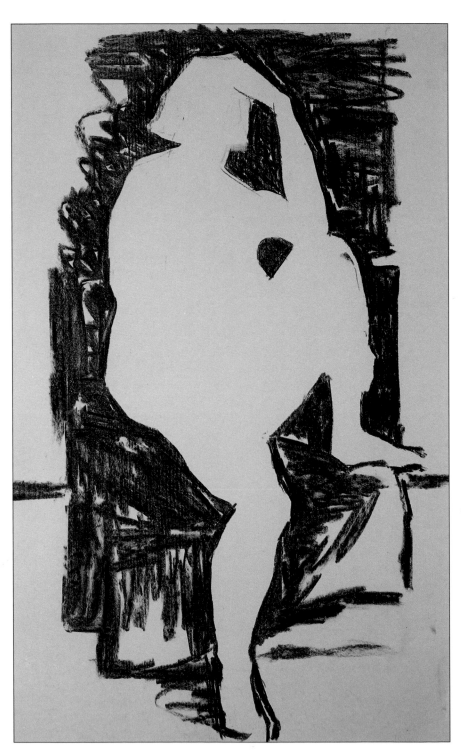

RIGHT **The completed drawing. The chair and the floor line have been indicated to keep the figure from "floating" in a void.**

DRAWING NEGATIVE SPACE

Using a soft pencil or charcoal, observe and draw one section of the background or negative space around a portion of the figure. Try to fill in the negative space with your pencil or charcoal without making a complete outline first. Use rapid strokes to make a dark shading. Work on one part of the body at a time. Give yourself enough time to observe carefully – you will need at least 30 minutes for each pose at first. Draw the chair or couch that the model is posing on, leaving the figure as a silhouette. You can now assess the quality of the design that the figure makes on the page, and if you are planning a composition you may wish to change your position to obtain a view of the model that will give you a more interesting shape to draw.

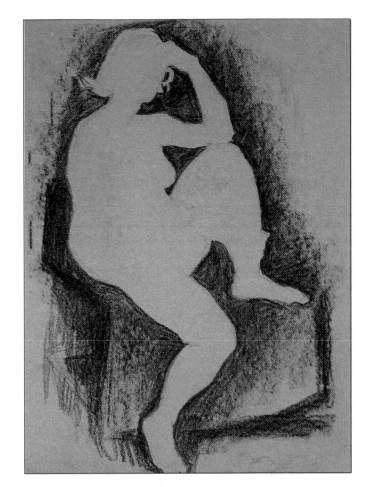

ABOVE RIGHT **A charcoal drawing on tinted pastel paper. The negative space has been so well observed that our eye can fill in the missing forms in the silhouette.**

RIGHT **The artist has used the negative space and architectural elements in this charcoal drawing to make a very interesting graphic design. The charcoal stick has been used on its side to make the gray shading.**

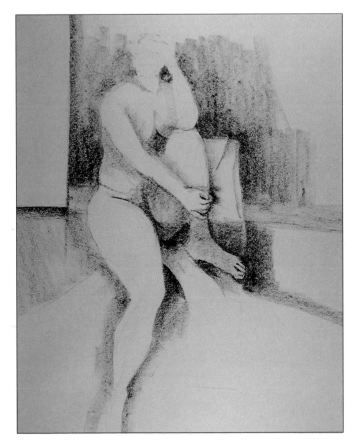

5

COORDINATION
OF HAND AND EYE

Good coordination of hand and eye is of fundamental importance in drawing. One of our most experienced models startled the class one day by saying that she knew which one of them would have the best drawing simply by watching them. "A professional painter glances at the paper and looks at the model, but students spend most of their time looking at their paper not the model." Embarrassment and self-consciousness may be partly to blame, but at the beginning we may have to force ourselves to look and observe in order to establish a proper coordination of our hand and eye.

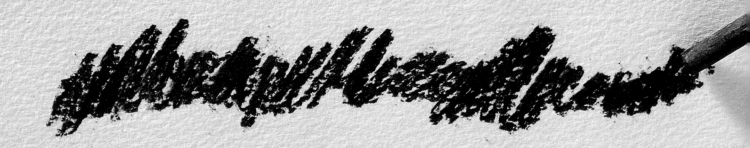

CONTOUR DRAWING

Contour drawing is the best method I know for achieving this coordination. It tackles the basic problem that occurs when you look at the paper too much when you draw and do not refer back to the figure. With contour drawing you reverse all of that. You look exclusively at the model without reference to the paper at all. The eye and pen are moved slowly around the contours of the body at the same speed, almost as if they were connected by a string.

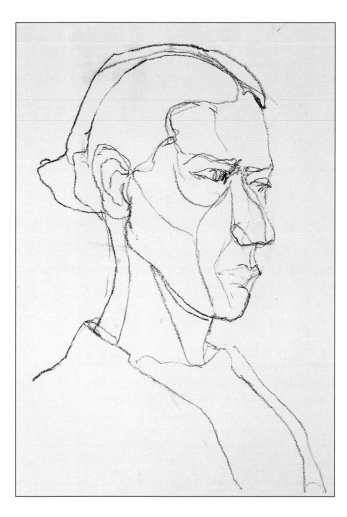

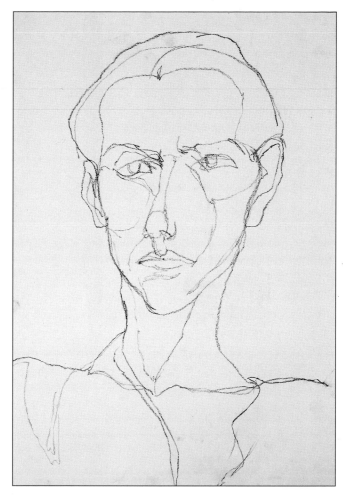

ABOVE LEFT AND RIGHT Charcoal contour portraits of the front and profile, exploring the planes as well as the contours of the face.

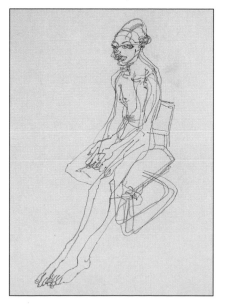

LEFT A contour drawing of a figure on a chair done with a drawing pen. The artist continued to draw over his first drawing as he searched for all of the forms.

EXERCISE IN CONTOUR DRAWING

A felt-tip pen or crayon is best for this exercise. You can draw all of the figure or, if you prefer, part of the figure so that you can concentrate on detail. Allowing yourself plenty of time, follow all the lines in the figure, keeping your eyes off the paper and on the model. You can glance at the paper to reposition your pen when you start drawing another part of the figure, then continue to draw without referring back to the paper. Obviously, the drawings will be grossly distorted, but this is not important – they are just exercises. After two hours, your observation and coordination should have improved.

You can continue your exercises in observation by doing contour drawings of still-life subjects or pieces of furniture. The principle is the same no matter what you are drawing. Henri Matisse (1869–1954) made contour drawing a regular part of his regime throughout his long career.

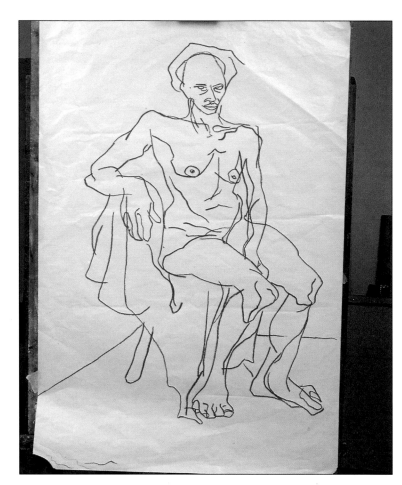

ABOVE **Although there is the usual distortion of a contour drawing, something of the essence of the** model has been captured by the careful and intensive observation.

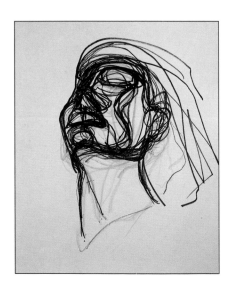

ABOVE AND RIGHT **These depictions of heads represent a different type of contour drawing. The eye was still kept on the model, but the felt-tip pen was moved quickly over the forms in an attempt to "feel" the planes of the face.**

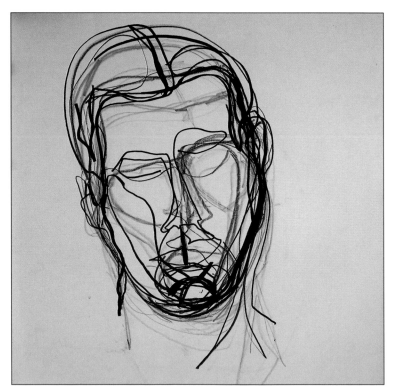

6
BALANCE

Balance and movement are two sides of the same coin. In reality, perfect balance is fleeting – the body is constantly making small adjustments to "hold" its balance. Balance can be thought of as a pause in movement.

The Italian artists gave us the term *contrapposto*, which means counterposing one part of the body against another to maintain a position in balance. For example, when a model stands with almost all her weight on one leg, the shoulders relax and drop down over the side of that leg. They counter the upward thrust of the hip. The head in turn tilts in the opposite direction to the shoulders. Thus protected from falling sideways, the model can hold her pose.

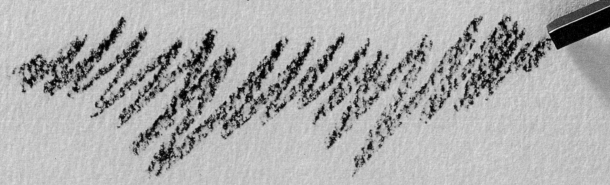

Movement occurs when we overreach our point of balance, whether accidentally or deliberately. It is important to grasp this fact because we must look for the flow of movement and the tension of muscles, even when the most professional of models is posing. Nothing is ever static in life – or in life drawing.

The correct line of balance in a pose must be established for two reasons. First and most obvious is the need to avoid a drawing in which the figure seems to be leaning or tilting. There is, however, a second, more subtle reason. A figure must look well-rooted and balanced if it is to seem to have a firm sense of mass and weight. Without this the drawing, although correct in other ways, will not be truly convincing.

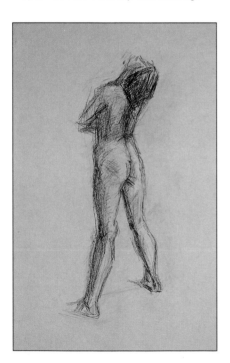

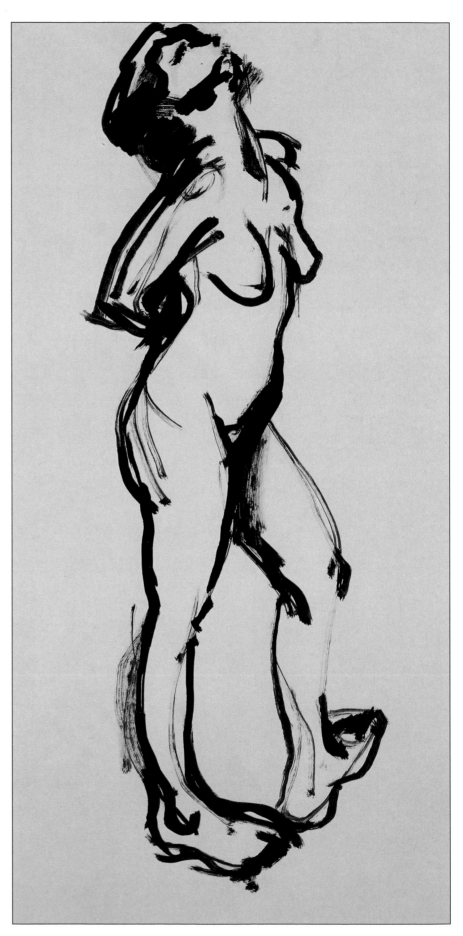

ABOVE **A pencil sketch in which the model has her weight on both feet. Her body arches forward to keep the balance point, here at the back of the neck, over her feet.**

RIGHT **In this quick brush and ink sketch, the model's body arches out to keep in balance. The balance line runs down from the back of the neck to the arch of the right foot.**

DETERMINING THE LINE OF BALANCE

In order to observe and measure balance, we use three points in the body through which we pass an imaginary plumb line. They are, first, from the front, the hollow space between the two clavicles (collarbones) at the pit of the neck; second, for a side or profile of the figure, from the ear hole; and finally, for a back view, from the middle of the base of the neck.

If you hold up a pencil vertically in your line of vision from one of those points, the imaginary plumb line will intersect the exact point on the ground where the weight of the body is falling. If, for example, the model has all her weight on one leg, the balance line will run from the balance point down the body to the arch of the foot carrying the weight. Because it is uncomfortable to stand with all your weight on one leg, it will be more likely that the model will be posed so that the weight is unevenly distributed, which will cause the balance line to fall somewhere between the feet.

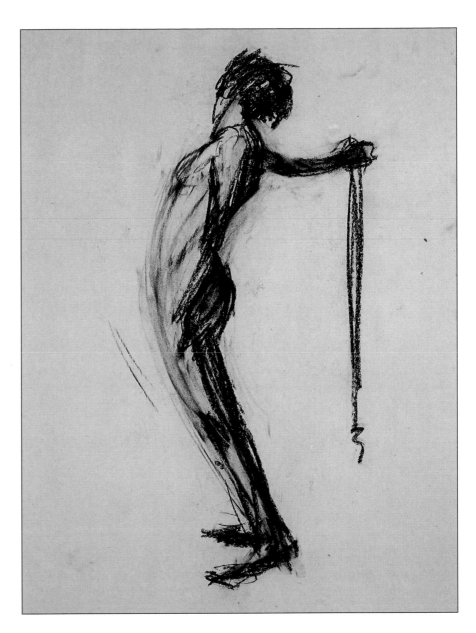

ABOVE **A quick charcoal sketch in which you can see how the body bows out and arches to maintain the balance point at the back of the neck over the feet.**

RIGHT **A pencil sketch clearly showing the balance point of the clavicle over the weight-bearing leg.**

FAR RIGHT **A pencil drawing showing how, as the body bends over, the balance point maintains its position directly above the weight-bearing legs.**

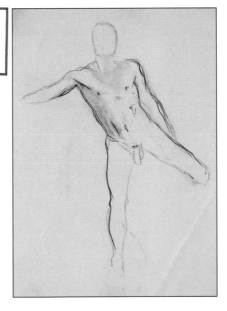

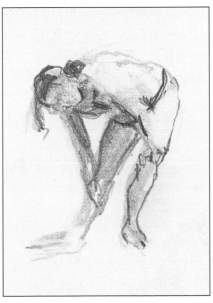

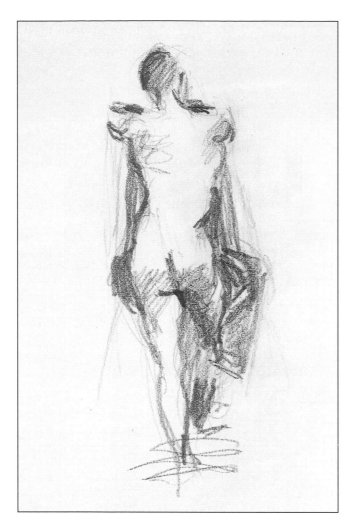

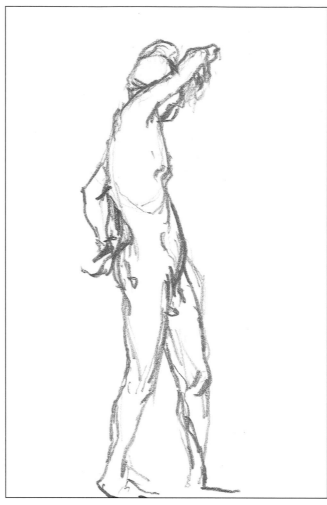

When you have determined this point by observing the model, draw a line vertically on your sheet, starting at the balance point. If it is a front pose, the starting point will be the hollow between the collarbones, and if the model's weight is wholly on one foot, the position of that foot on the ground will be directly on the line. If, as is more likely, her weight is distributed between the feet, mark their position in relation to the balance line.

Once you have determined where the weight is falling, observe the hips and shoulders. If the model's weight is mainly on one leg, that hip will be pushed up and the shoulder above it will slope down to counterbalance the thrust of the hip. This *contrapposto* is essential for

ABOVE LEFT **In this pencil sketch the balance point at the back of the neck is directly over the leg that is carrying the weight.**

ABOVE RIGHT **A pencil sketch showing how, even when the body twists around, the balance point remains over the leg bearing the weight.**

balance. The body is, in fact, most unstable when it is standing rigidly upright; it maintains equilibrium automatically by compensating for the thrust of one part with the opposing movement of another part.

This is evident when you look at the back of a model posing with her weight on one foot: her spine curves as it comes down from the neck and shoulders, the curve continues through the pelvis, which is pushed up on the weight-bearing hip, and down the leg to the arch of the foot. The counterthrust of spine, hip, and leg forms an S-shaped curve. This reverse curve is called Rubens's S, after the old master who used it so effectively in many of his drawings and paintings.

USING THE BALANCE LINE FROM THE SIDE

J U S T I N   J O N E S

This is an example of how to find the balance line of a standing figure when you can only see the side profile of the model. The balance point is measured from the ear hole, and the weight of the body will fall directly from this point.

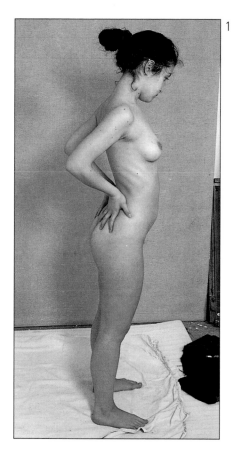

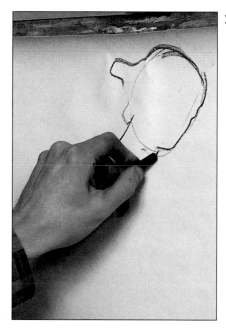

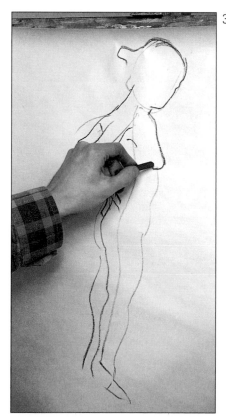

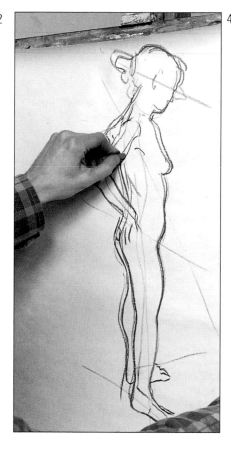

1 Although the model's body bows forward, the balance point of her ear hole stays over the two feet carrying her weight.

2 The artist roughly indicates the shape and direction of the head.

3 The artist has lightly drawn a balance line from the ear to the feet, establishing the position of the body.

4 Additional guidelines for the direction of the head, the thrust of the pelvis, and the position of the feet on the floor have been added. The artist is now able to complete this drawing, adding color with pastel pencil.

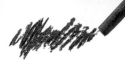

FINDING THE CORRECT BALANCE FROM THE FRONT

DIANA CONSTANCE

When the model is facing you, the balance line is drawn downward from the clavicle; that is the point between the two collarbones. If the model has her weight on one leg, the balance line will pass through the arch of that foot. If the weight is divided between the legs, the line will intersect a point between the feet.

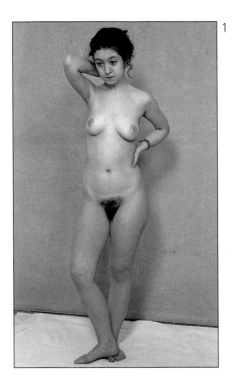

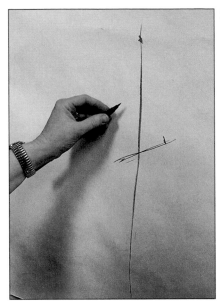

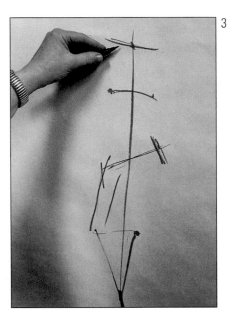

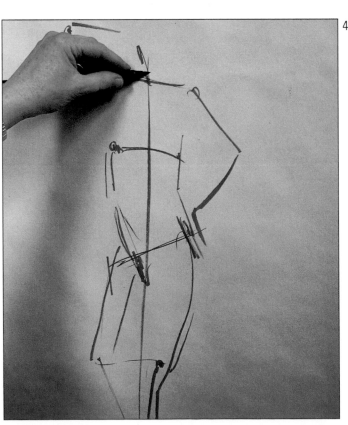

1 The model has been asked to assume a pose with her weight completely on one leg, which is very uncomfortable and can only be held for a few minutes.

2 The vertical balance line is put in first, and then a guideline is drawn across the hips. The weight is on the right leg, causing the hip on that side to be pushed up.

3 A guideline is now drawn across the shoulders and breast, showing the tilt of the shoulders downward over the weight-bearing right hip. The position of the legs is indicated.

4 The counter-thrust of the head and neck are added; these counter movements lock the body into a sustainable balance.

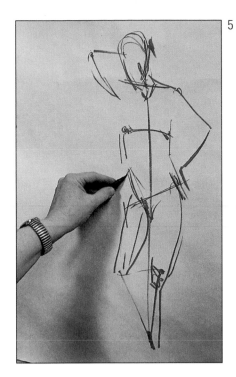

5 The form of the body begins to emerge, firmly held in the right position by the guidelines.

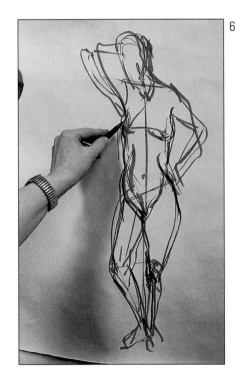

6 An additional felt-tip pen of another color is used to explore the forms and reinforce the drawing.

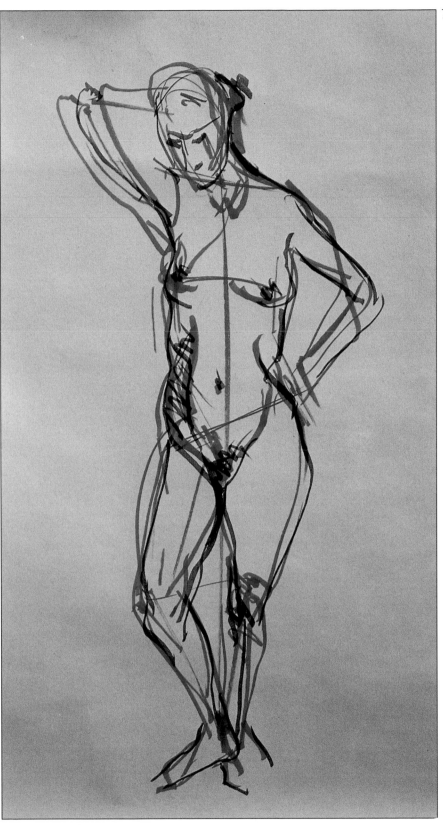

7 This is a quick demonstration to show how the balance of the figure is set out. A nonerasable felt-tip pen would not be used in a normal drawing, where the guidelines would be lightly drawn in.

⁊

MOVEMENT

How often have you heard a fine drawing admired because it "seems to be alive"? Good drawings give the illusion of life, and implying movement is one part of this.

The movement of a pose flows through the whole of the body. It is impossible to move one part of the figure without causing a chain of reactions in all the other muscles, as they make minute adjustments to maintain the body's balance. This contraction and elongation of the muscles form the rhythmical pattern by which we maintain our equilibrium. Even when the model is perfectly still, her body is held in the pose by a network of counterbalancing muscles. This is why, with even the most relaxed pose, a model needs to rest after 45 minutes or an hour.

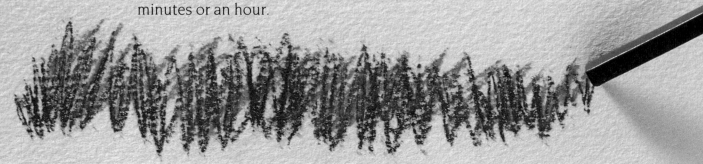

Everybody holds themselves and moves in a wholly individual way. It is often possible to recognize someone at a distance by the way he or she is walking, long before you can see the face. Body language is very important in drawing – it can say more about people than they may want you to know. Tense people contract their muscles, bunching up and compressing their bodies as if they are "holding something in." The lines tend to be angular, with the arms and limbs crossed and held tightly. Relaxed people make long,

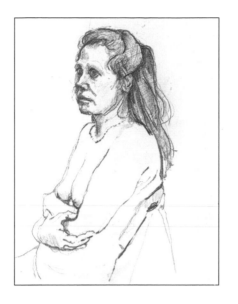

flowing lines and strides when they move. Their elongated muscle forms curves, and their joints are loose. This body language is a form of "still" movement, and it is very expressive of mood and personality.

LEFT AND BELOW The pencil drawing (left) shows the girl's tightly contained, negative energy. Compare this with the almost feline energy of the man in the picture below, poised as if about to spring.

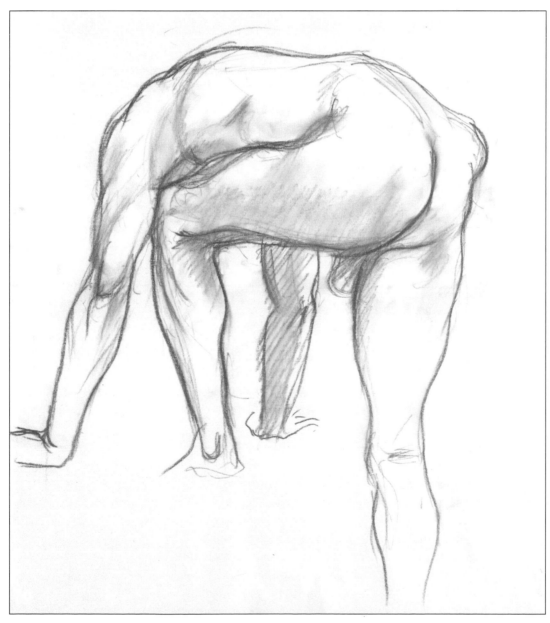

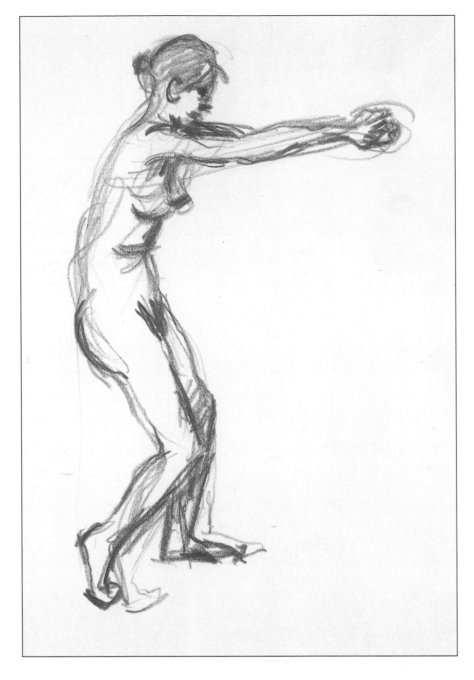

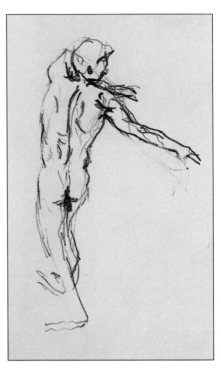

ABOVE **The model is slightly off-balance as he swings around.**

Movement such as walking or running is a controlled loss of balance. As we step forward, the center of gravity of our body is moved forward, we lose our balance for a split second, and our leg moves from behind to catch us. As long as the balance of the body is kept forward, the movement is repeated and on we go, walking, first losing our balance, then regaining it. If you want to draw a person running or leaping or otherwise in motion, be sure to place the balance point slightly ahead of the direction of the movement, so that it shows the body at that critical point when it is slightly out of balance. Then the figure will look as if it were just caught in motion.

In this lesson we will dispense with worries about proportion and detail and instead try to concentrate completely on movement. Look for the major line of the movement in the pose and let the rest follow on.

CAPTURING MOVEMENT

Ask the model to move as if she were in slow motion. Using charcoal or a felt-tip pen, follow her movements with one continuous line. Try keeping your pen or charcoal on the paper all the time. Move up and down the form, crossing over from one part of the body to another with a continuous line. The aim is to build up a spontaneous, natural rhythm, so do not stop to make corrections: draw over a line if necessary. The object is to see and draw only the flow of the figure.

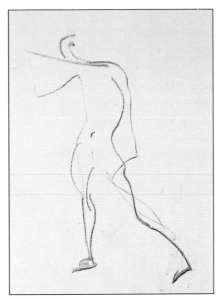

A B O V E **A 30-second pose, in which the line is brought all the way through the figure to show the pure movement.**

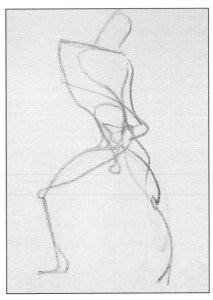

A B O V E **A 30-second pose. The artist is not drawing the contours of the body. Instead, the quick line moves across and down the figure to capture the movement.**

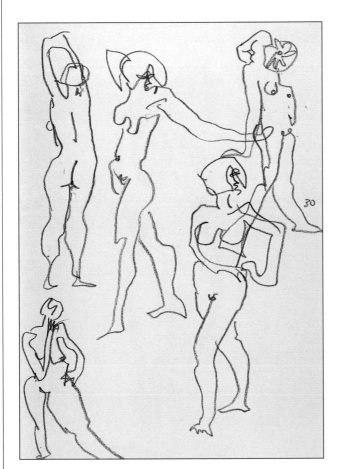

A B O V E **A page of quick sketches where the contours of the figures are loosely drawn with a felt-tip pen.**

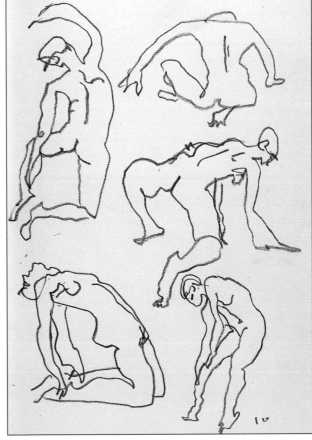

A B O V E **Although these drawings are all done in less than a minute, relating the shapes and movements of the figures makes an interesting overall pattern.**

LONGER POSES

After about 15 minutes of slow-motion drawings, increase the time allowed to one-minute poses. As before, look for the major movement of the figure first. Then carry on, slowly increasing the amount of information that you have time to put into the drawing. Continue to increase the time very gradually by having five-minute poses for at least half an hour. Take care not to lose the flow of movement by slowing down and becoming tentative.

Changing the medium to brush and ink is an interesting variation in this study of movement. It will increase the need to be quick and decisive in the five-minute poses.

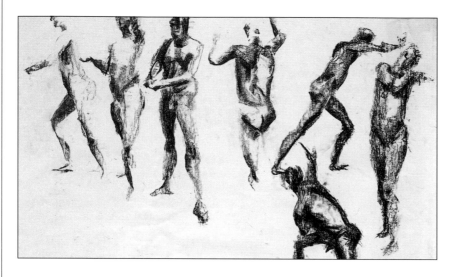

LEFT This is a page of charcoal drawings showing the play of light on an almost continuously moving figure.

BELOW LEFT A felt-tip pen is the perfect medium to make a shorthand note of the long, fluid lines of a quick pose.

BELOW RIGHT A Chinese brush and ink are used here to bold effect, describing both the movement and fleshy quality of the model.

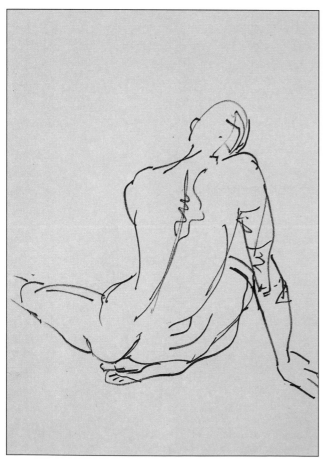

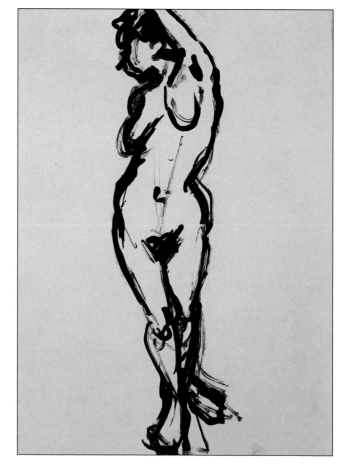

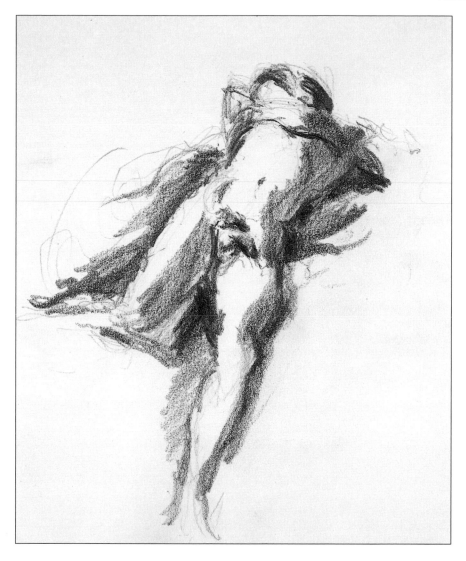

LEFT A quick sketch done with graphite. The end of the stick has been sharpened to a wedge point with a mat knife. This enables the artist to use the broad edge quickly to draw in the negative space around the figure. The point is then rotated to the sharp end for the fine, crisp lines. This is an effective way to make a very complete note of a moving figure. Although the body is only indicated, it convinces us of its movement and weight by the use of the negative space.

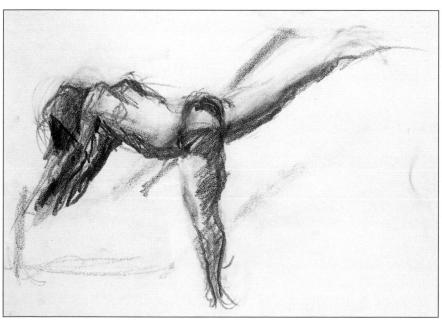

LEFT The model is in almost continuous movement for this drawing, and the artist needs to work very quickly. He draws rapidly with a graphite stick. In this situation the details of the figure are completely ignored, and all of the energy is spent in catching the movement.

8

THE ILLUSION OF SPACE

The abiity to draw three-dimensionally does not occur naturally. A child, for example, will draw an object's height and width, but not its depth. We can rely on a certain instinctive sense of color and design, but when it comes to drawing an image three-dimensionally, we must oppose our natural tendency to draw in two dimensions.

The Italian architect Filippo Brunelleschi (1377–1446) developed the mathematical basics of perspective. He was able to imagine the possibility of changing a flat, insubstantial piece of paper into a palazzo or landscape of infinitesimal depth. However, although Brunelleschi is generally credited with starting the obsession with space in western art, the recent discovery of a rare wall painting, depicting the rape of Persephone, in the Macedonian royal tombs, suggests that Greek painters in the 4th century B.C. understood and used three-dimensional foreshortening. This means that perspective may have been used by Greek mathematicians 2,000 years before the Renaissance. Whomever we have to thank, the ability to introduce depth to a flat surface has been of fundamental importance and changed western art.

Drawing the human body in perspective is vastly more complex than a building or landscape since the structure is constantly changing. In order to draw a foreshortened figure and put it into a composition, we need to understand a few basic rules of perspective.

BELOW The illusion of space is created in this drawing by the foot thrusting out toward the viewer. The subtle use of a cast shadow across the abdomen enhances the feeling of light and space.

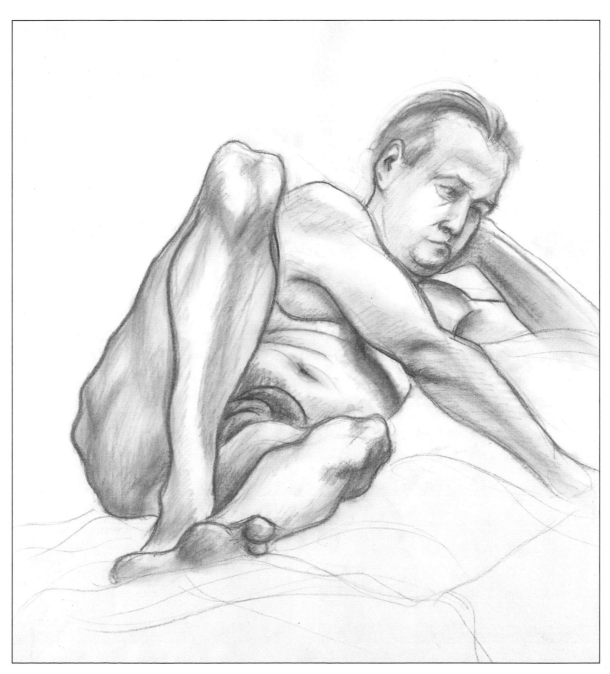

UNDERSTANDING PERSPECTIVE

The floor that you stand on in the studio is what we call the ground plane. If you were outside on flat ground, you could see the ground plane stretching away from you until it reached the horizon. Try holding up a pencil horizontally in front of your eyes. You will notice that this line is exactly on the horizon. So what we refer to as the horizon corresponds exactly with our eye level. If you sit down, the horizon moves down with the level of your eyes; as you stand up, eye level and the horizon move upward.

The same thing happens in a studio, but inside a room we are less aware of the horizon and hence of eye level. Check the eye level of the pose. If you are sitting down and the model is lying on a couch, she may be directly at eye level. If, however, you are standing up at an easel, the model will be below eye level. If the person beside you is sitting down and you are standing up at an easel, you will each produce a very different drawing of the same pose.

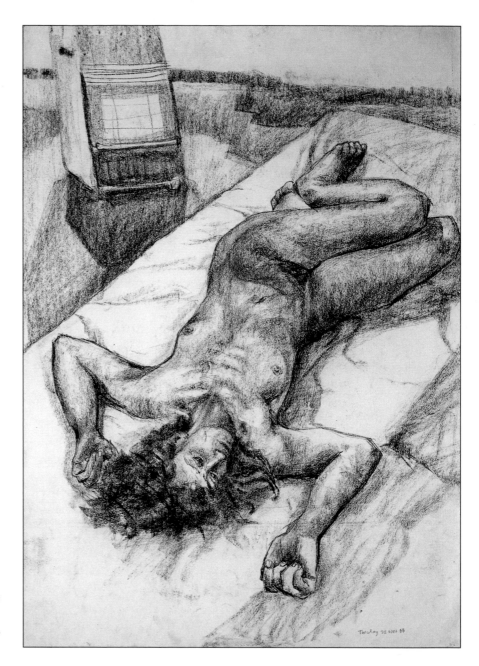

RIGHT **The model is below the eye level of the artist. The perspective of the drawing is helped by drawing her in the context of the room.**

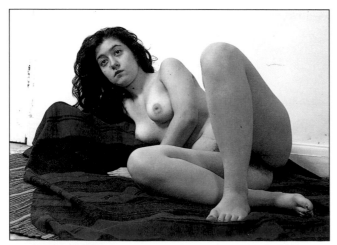

ABOVE **The model seen at eye level.**

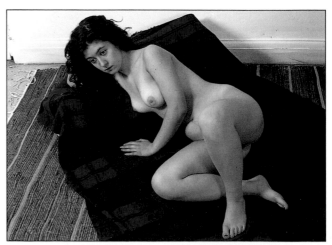

ABOVE **The same pose with the model below eye level.**

Determining eye level

When the model has assumed the pose, look at the wall or area behind her. Keep your head straight and do not look up or down at the model. Hold your pencil horizontally in front of your eyes – this is your eye level. Take note where the pencil is in relation to the model and the wall behind her. If the pencil crosses the figure, she is at eye level; if she is lying down and the pencil is above the model, she is below eye level; if she is sitting on a high stool, the pencil may be on a line below part of her, and she will be partially or wholly above your eye level.

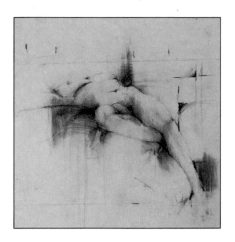

RIGHT A simple pencil line and crosshatching has been used to create a feeling of three-dimensional space. The top part of the body has been allowed to fade back into the distance. The planes of the body are used to show the twist between the legs and pelvis.

Measuring the foreshortened figure

The body assumes odd shapes in a foreshortened pose. We tend to mistrust our eyes, and draw what we think we see and not what is actually in front of us. To avoid this, the artist uses careful measurement to make sure of objective observation. Start with the traditional method of measurement. Hold a pencil with outstretched arm, line up the end of the pencil with one part of the model's body, and use your thumb to mark the length of that part on the pencil. This will allow you to compare the proportions and distance between the different parts of the body. If you are going to measure their relationships precisely, you must remember to stand in exactly the same spot; any movement will change your angle to the pose and affect the measurements.

You can also use the method of drawing and measuring the negative space around the figure. The term negative space refers to the area surrounding the figure (see page 28). If the model is lying down, draw the shape of the rug or drapery under her; it is often easier to see the pose from the outside of the figure.

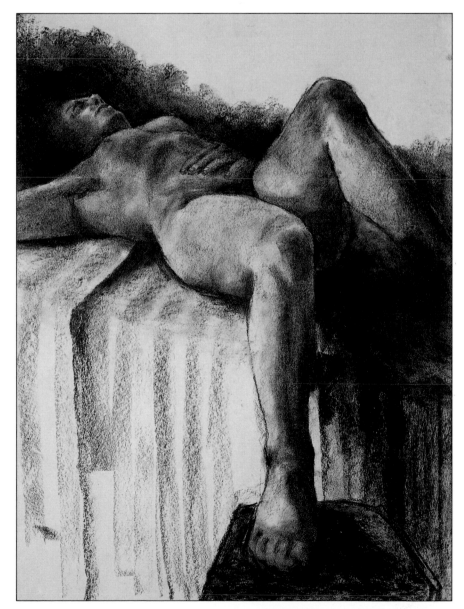

ABOVE This effective charcoal drawing was done close up to the model, and it has the typical distortion caused by extreme foreshortening.

Drawing the foreshortened figure

Before we can draw a foreshortened figure and put it into a composition, we need to understand a few basic rules of perspective. To learn how to draw the figure three-dimensionally, we will begin with geometric shapes that represent the different parts of the body. It is useful to draw a rectangle and cylinder in perspective and to learn how to turn and represent these shapes at different eye levels.

I would suggest that at this stage you draw a diagrammatic sketch using the geometric shapes to simplify and clarify the foreshortened pose. Check your observation by looking at the negative space and measuring. There is always the temptation to make a figure that is lying down stand up. This is the result of a mistake with the perspective of the eye level. A part of the body that is closer to you will appear much larger, while the shapes will diminish in size as they recede. The closer you are to the model, the

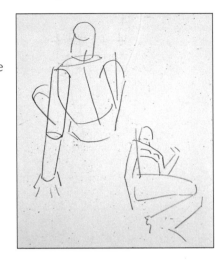

ABOVE **The body has been sketched in, using simple geometric shapes. This method can be a help when you begin to draw the foreshortened figure.**

more pronounced this effect will be. It is like taking a photograph with a wide-angle lens: objects close to the lens appear gigantic compared with the other objects. Artists often draw the part of the body that is closest to them with a darker line or in greater detail to bring it forward. Exaggerated foreshortening is frequently used to good effect to increase the depth in the picture plane.

OPPOSITE ABOVE **A charcoal sketch of a figure with a split eye level: the top part of this figure is at eye level, but the leg falls below eye level.**

OPPOSITE BELOW **A simplified drawing of the finished work directly above.**

BELOW **When a figure is reduced to geometric shapes, we can see how the lower leg is drawn below eye level. The curve of the body comes up onto a flat plane, which is at the artist's eye level.**

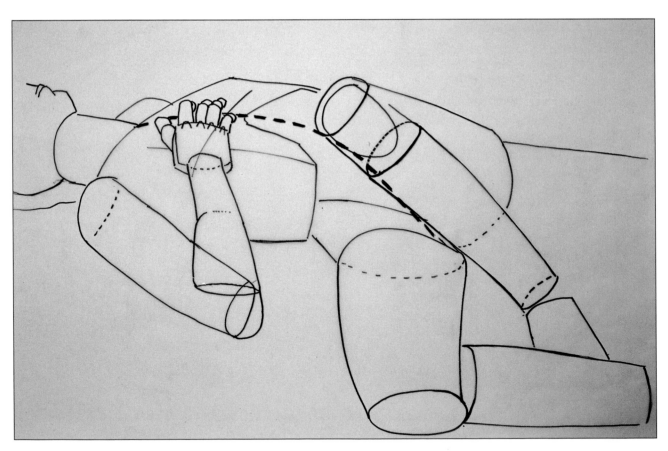

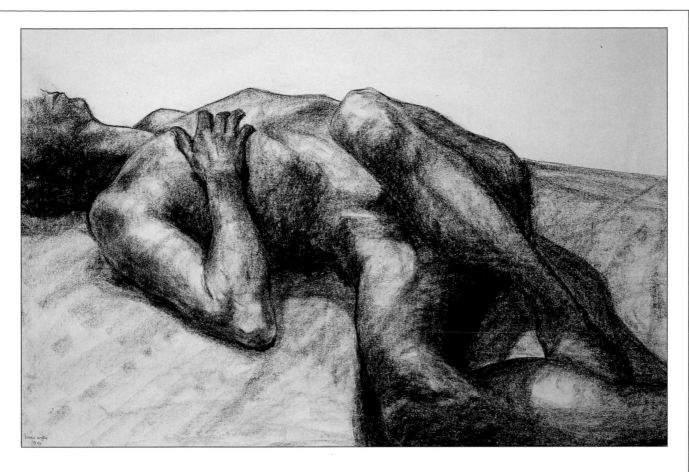

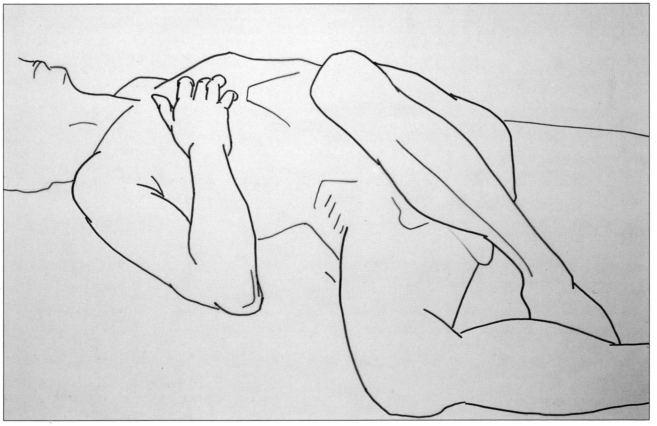

DRAWING THE FORESHORTENED FIGURE

J U S T I N   J O N E S

A systematic approach is necessary when drawing a foreshortened pose. We have a preconceived image of what the body should look like. The distortions caused by foreshortening run counter to this notion. Allow yourself at least twice the time you would need for a normal pose so that you can make careful measurements – and then trust them.

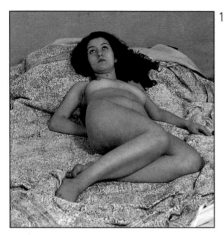

1 The model is posed on the floor so that she can be drawn just below the artist's eye level.

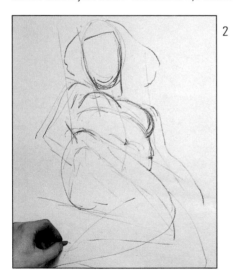

2 The artist has begun by using guidelines to give him the direction of the forms. He is working all over the figure and not concentrating on details.

3 The basic drawing of the model is complete. Note how the important depth of the thigh has been drawn through as a cylinder.

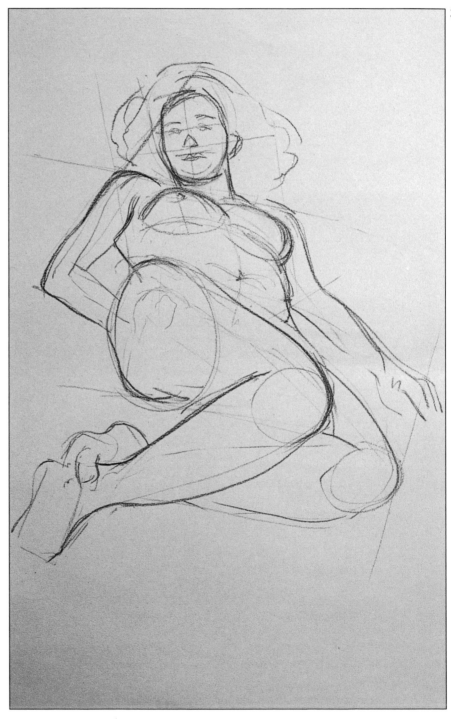

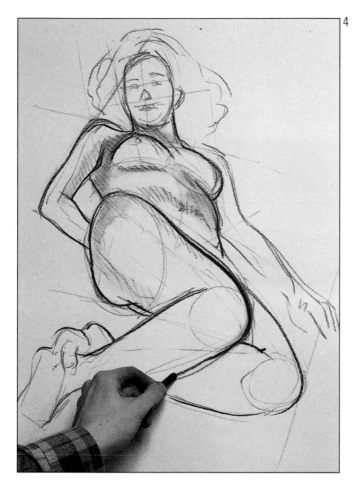

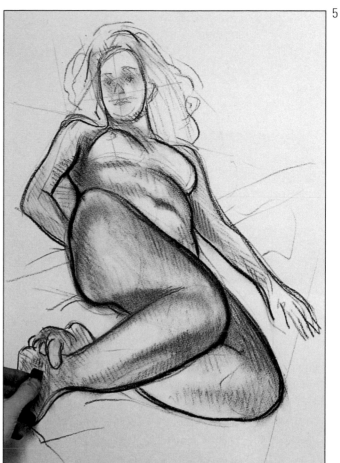

4 The artist uses a conte stick to strengthen the lines of the drawing and begin the modeling.

5 The artist is enhancing the modeling of the figure, working from the limbs in the foreground.

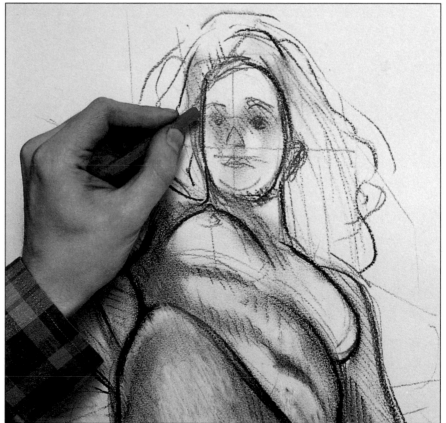

6 Note how the breasts are drawn on the curved surface of the rib cage.

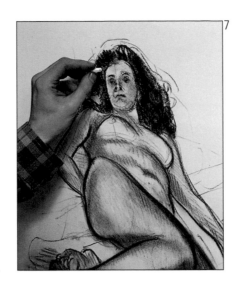

7 The artist finishes the details of the face and the hair at the last stage of the drawing.

8 The completed drawing. You can see how the artist has drawn the size of the forms, diminishing as they recede.

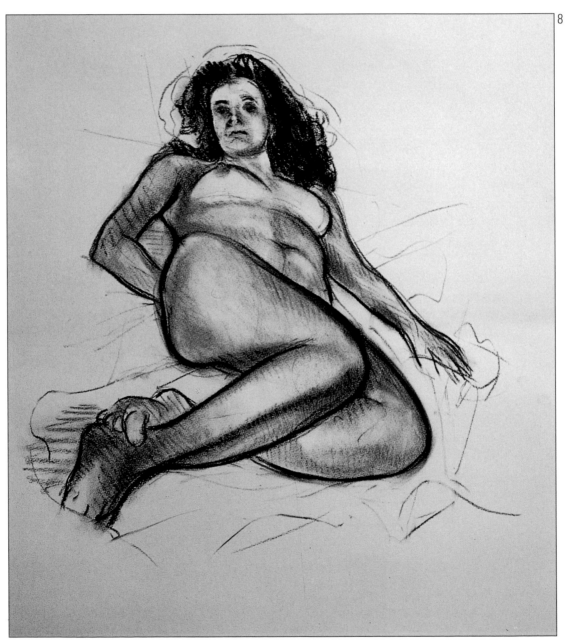

LIGHT

Light can have a magical effect, transforming an intrinsically dull subject into a fascinating image. I regard the five years that I spent studying and working as a photographer as the most valuable experience that I have had as a painter. In photography you quickly become aware that what you are seeing and trying to photograph is completely dependent on the light, and the quality of light often matters more than the subject. On one memorable occasion, I arrived very early in the morning to photograph a site in northern Greece, but by the time the officials had been summoned and the paperwork completed, it was midday. The sun by then was directly overhead, bleaching out the ruins, and the marble columns were standing in their own shadow. There was nothing to do but pack up and go.

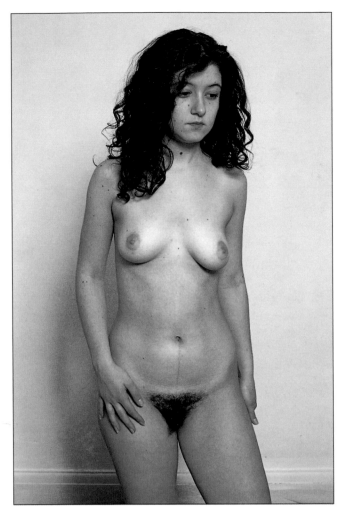

ABOVE **Flat overhead lighting.**

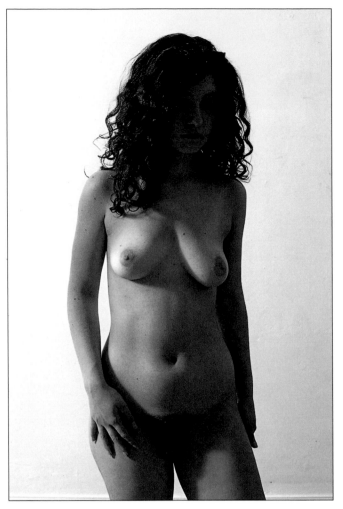

ABOVE **Harsh side lighting.**

When we look at a model, what we actually see is the light being reflected from her body and the area around it. If you change the lighting, you have a different image. The light changes the abstract composition in the pose by making the planes of the body more apparent, casting shadows and highlighting areas that become more important visually. Light also has a profound effect on the mood of the drawing.

An overall flat light is sufficient for a line drawing in which you want to see the contours of the figure clearly. However, in order to model the form, try arranging the light differently. This need not involve great changes – simply turn off some of the lights on one side of the

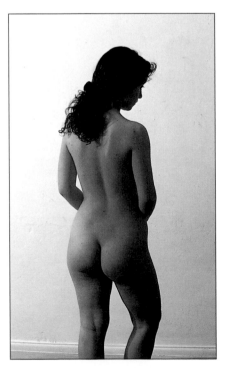

ABOVE **A soft bounced lighting.**

room, for example, to give a softer, directed light with shadows. There are advantages to using a dim light: it does not flatten the form, and it enables you to observe the subtle shading of the body for modeling. A harsh light, on the other hand, will change the mood and create strong patterns of light and shade. The long shadows that are cast can be used to create depth in the picture plane. A simple spotlight is a welcome addition to any studio. It can be directed onto the model to give a strong, dramatic effect, or it can be bounced off a wall or a sheet of canvas to give a soft, reflected light. Introducing a simple floor or table lamp can completely change a pose and help a composition.

MODELING WITH LIGHT

The possibilities of lighting are generally underestimated, which is unfortunate, because working with light can be an important means of developing your work. Modeling tones of light and shadow is a quite different kind of drawing from using line. This is not meant as a criticism of line, for there is a unique purity and lyricism in a fine line drawing that cannot be equalled by the heavier techniques of modeling. However, modeling brings us a step closer to representing the reality of what we see. Line may be regarded as an extension of writing. As we draw, the line envelopes and "describes" the form in a literate and poetic sense, but it stands back from trying to copy nature. When we look for the highlights, middle tones, and shadows on a figure, we are striving towards an approximation of nature, "to draw as we see."

Curiously, it is difficult and unnatural to work in this way. In general, people feel happier when they are putting lines around a figure, but sometimes these lines proliferate and become scribble lines or crosshatching. When this happens, the simple line becomes a tone and forms a bridge between the extremes of line and modeling.

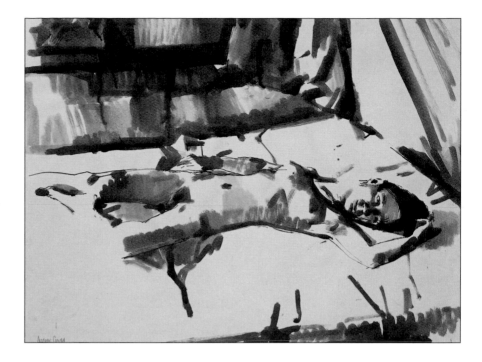

ABOVE **This sensitive dark sepia wash creates the illusion of light flooding the room so that the model becomes an abstract pattern of shapes. A Chinese brush was used.**

BELOW **The body is caught in a delicate web of thin charcoal line. The darker shades have been built up in a negative space to contrast with the body, which seems to glow with light.**

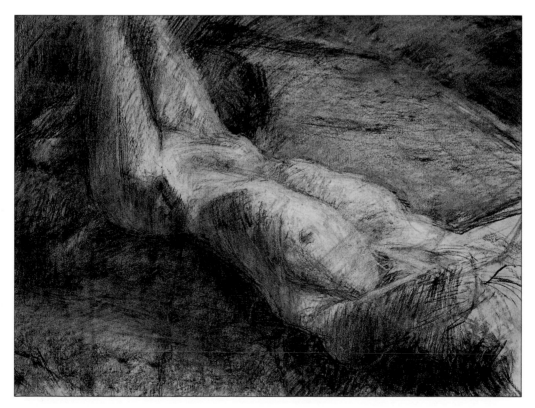

MODELING WITH SOFT PASTELS ON TINTED PAPER

This lesson is intended as a first step to modeling the figure. Giving up line for tone is quite a change, and I would suggest that in the beginning you use a small spotlight to help you see the areas of light and shadow on the figure. You will gradually develop an eye for the planes of the body.

Start by drawing just the light falling on the body. Work with short poses – one minute, say – and use a very soft light pastel on tinted or dark paper. Colored or tinted pastel paper is ideal, but any dark paper that has enough texture to hold the pastel will do. Try to catch the simple overall picture of light on the figure, and avoid breaking up the pattern of light and movement by drawing the small, irrelevant shapes. There is usually one dominant light area on a figure, so look for this first.

The pressure you exert on the pastel will determine the depth of tone or color. Hold the stick on the side and move it over the colored paper, varying the pressure on the pastel to create different depths of tone. In this case, the more strongly you press, the lighter the tone, and as you ease back the pressure, the pastel will leave a middle tone.

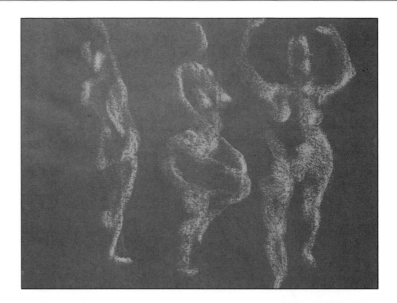

RIGHT ABOVE **In these 30-second poses, soft, ivory-colored pastel was used on tinted paper. The different light tones were made by slightly changing the pressure on the pastel.**

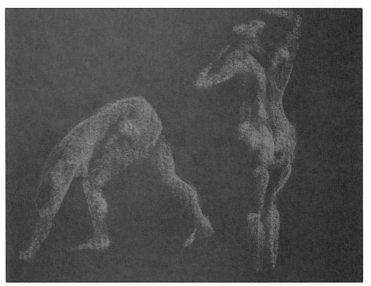

RIGHT MIDDLE AND BELOW **The poses have now been increased to one minute. The stick of soft pastel is held at an angle of approximately 45 degrees to the paper, with the point on the outside of the form. The point and angle of the pastel create a strong edge and tone simultaneously and allow you to catch the light and fluid movements quickly.**

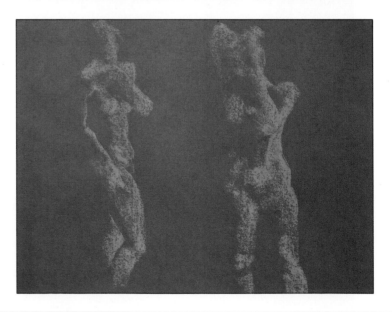

When you have completed a number of quick poses, increase the time to 30 minutes. You can now try drawing the shadow area on the figure as well as the light. Choose a pastel that is much darker than the tone of the paper you are working on. This time start the drawing with the dark shadows on the figure. When you have a complete pattern of the dark tones, add the highlights. If you wish, part of the tint of the paper can be left to show through on the figure so that it can work as a middle tone between dark and light.

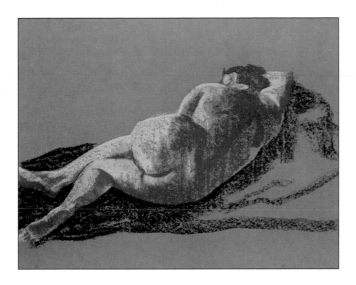

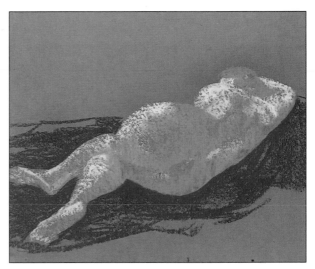

ABOVE LEFT AND RIGHT Two versions of the same pose. In both cases the light was drawn first. On the left, dark pastel in the shadow area creates a solid form. The bright orange used in the shadows for the right-hand version, makes the figure seem translucent.

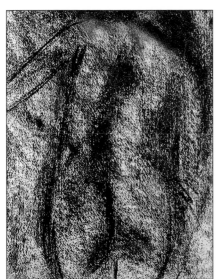

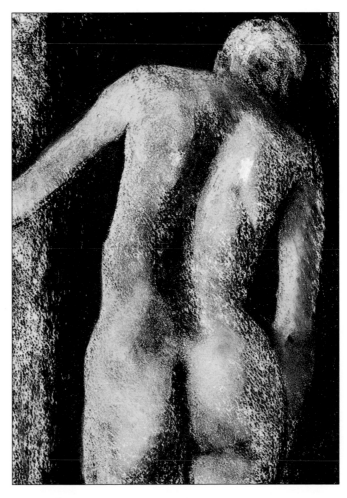

ABOVE AND RIGHT The paper was rubbed with charcoal before the drawing was made (above). The right-hand picture shows the completed drawing with soft ivory pastel in the lights and black pastel in the negative space.

MODELING WITH PASTEL IN SOFT LIGHT

D I A N A   C O N S T A N C E

The model was lying below the artist's eye level and was softly lit. A soft, warm gray shade of pastel was chosen to best express the subtle light. Ingres paper was used for its fine texture, which allows even blending of the pastel.

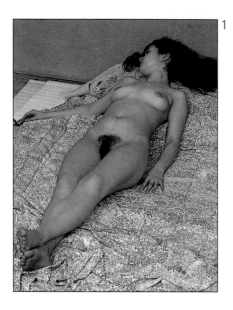

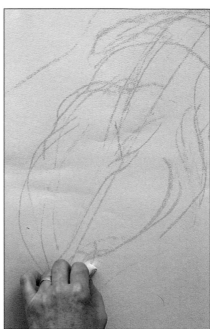

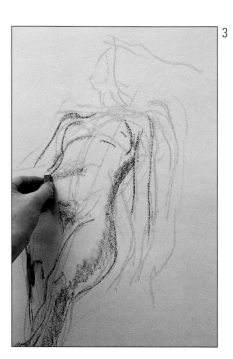

1 The model is lying below eye level. A soft light was achieved by bouncing the light of a "spot" off a white canvas.

2 A placement drawing is made with a pale pastel. Note the guidelines down the middle of the figure and across the chest, giving direction.

3 Once the placement and adjustments have been made, the darker pastel is added, using both the edge and side of the stick.

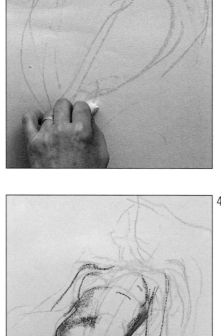

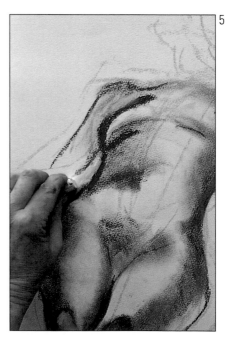

4 The thumb is used to begin the blending of the pastel. Some people prefer to use their hands rather than a blending stick.

5 Detail of the artist blending the pastel.

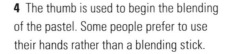

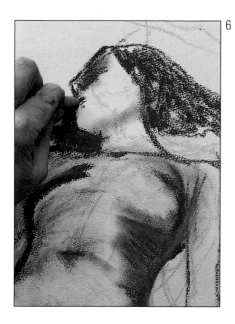

6

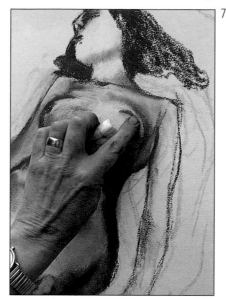

7

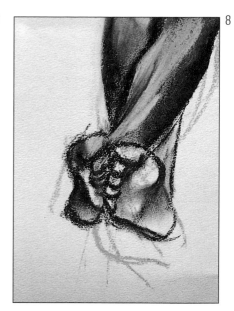

8

6 The hair is drawn up and over the form of the skull and underneath the left side of the face, which defines the shape of the head in the simplest terms.

7 Further modeling of the form is shown here. By using your finger, you can push the pastel into the paper, whereas a blending stick rubs a great deal of it off the paper.

8 A detail of the feet showing the strong modeling.

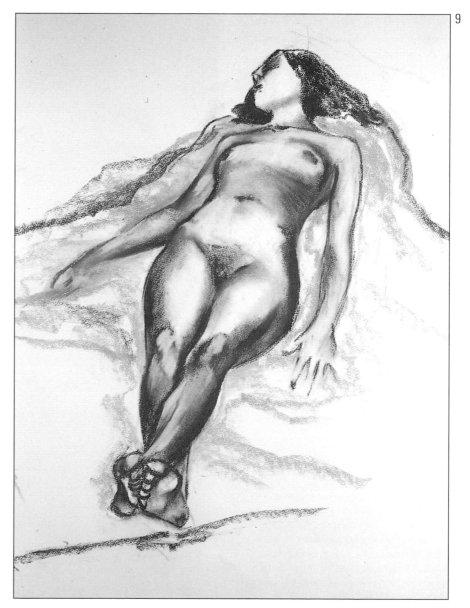

9

9 The completed drawing. The guidelines have been erased with fresh bread, and the drape has been added so that the model is not left floating.

THE EMERGENCE OF LIGHT THROUGH LINE

In an ideal world, the model would always be beautifully lit, and your job of modeling the figure would be simple. Unfortunately, the lighting in most studios is more appropriate to a supermarket than a studio for painting and drawing, and it is, therefore, essential to learn how to analyze the volume and shape of the model independent from the light source. This lesson is designed to help you imagine where the light would be on the figure.

The first step is to appreciate the volume and mass of the body. You will be working like a sculptor, but using a multitude of lines instead of a chisel to analyze the shapes. In trying to recreate the three-dimensional aspect of the form, you will have to decide which part of the figure is receding and which part comes forward to catch the light. The multiple lines are used to make a type of relief map of the body, rather in the way that a computer scans mountains and plains.

The lines will slowly build up and become darker until they exclude all but the strongest highlights that would be reflected from the figure. When the drawing is completed, it will demonstrate how you can show the emergence of light by using line alone.

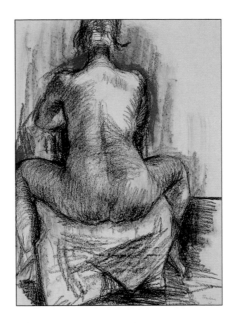

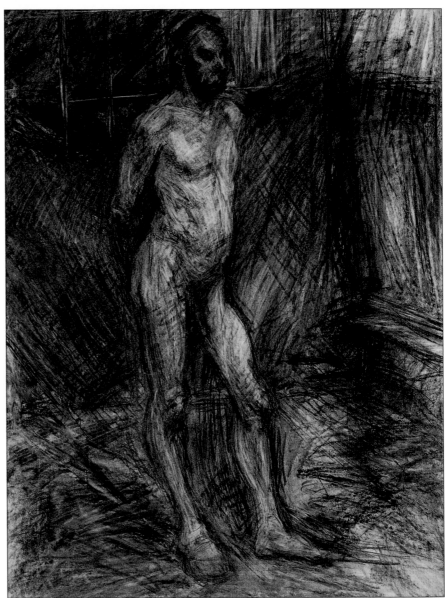

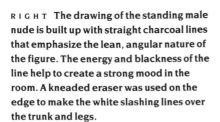

RIGHT **The drawing of the standing male nude is built up with straight charcoal lines that emphasize the lean, angular nature of the figure. The energy and blackness of the line help to create a strong mood in the room. A kneaded eraser was used on the edge to make the white slashing lines over the trunk and legs.**

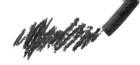

CREATING THE FORM THROUGH LINE

D I A N A   C O N S T A N C E

In this drawing of a simple pose, the technique of building up the volume and mass of the body using lines is demonstrated. Charcoal was used with some soft pastel added to the background in the early stages.

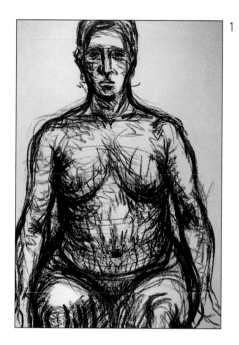

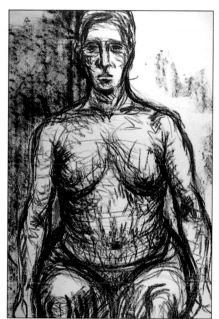

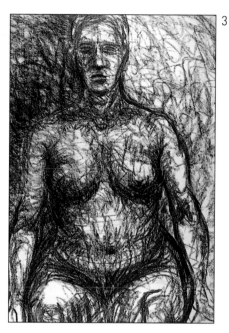

1 The model was asked to take a simple pose. The aim is to use the charcoal line as a sculptor would use a tool, going around the form many times to carve out and refine the directions of each part.

2 Soft pastel has been added to the background to bring out the figure.

3 A scribble line has been used in the background and on the figure in the shadow areas to deepen the tone. As the lines build up, the feeling of volume increases.

4 The envelopment of the figure by shadow is complete – only the highlights on the form are left. The drawing can be stopped at any point, and the more you continue to add lines, the more the model will slowly disappear into the darkness.

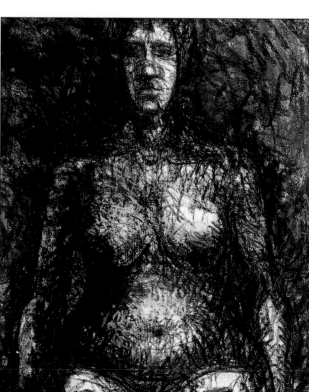

THE PLANES OF THE BODY

Although the body is composed of complicated, rounded shapes, artists frequently refer to the "planes" of a figure. There are three reasons for this apparent anomaly. First, the artist needs a shorthand method of simplifying and expressing these complex forms. Second, the artist needs to give the figure a strong three-dimensional quality. Third, the use of the plane and angle improves the composition and overcomes the problem of design by providing a contrast to curves and rounded forms in the body. Many artists use the planes in the body to increase the tension and graphic design element of a composition, and the use of angularity may be clearly seen in, for example, the work of Egon Schiele (1890–1918). As I have pointed out, true planes seldom exist in the body; we are looking for an approximation. There is a side of the thigh; a flat of the chest and shoulder blade; an angle of the elbow, ankle, or rib; the sharp cheekbone, and so on. The more angular and flat areas of the body are set against the round and curvaceous parts. The clearer the contrast between the two, the stronger will be the design.

To begin with, you will find it easier to draw the planes of the body when you are using some form of directed light. As you gain experience, this will not be as necessary.

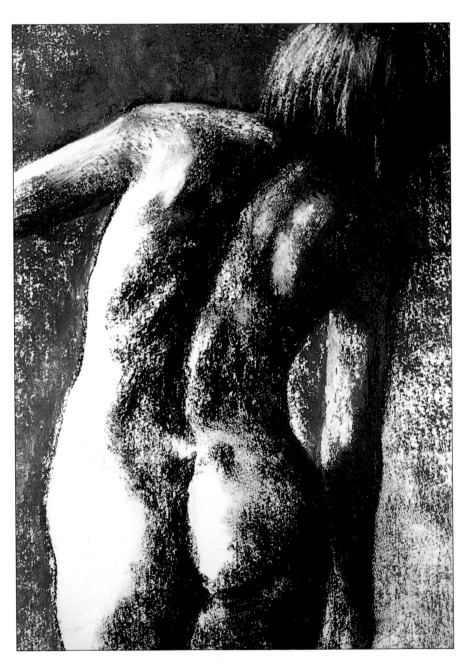

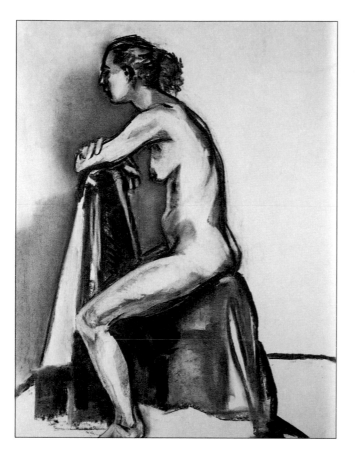

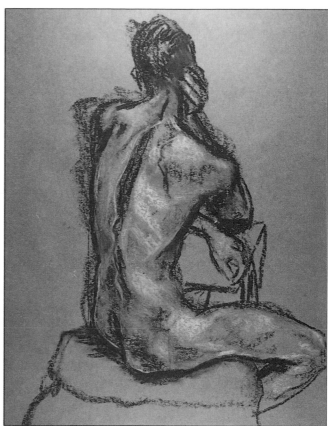

ABOVE In this charcoal drawing, the shadows have been blended.

ABOVE RIGHT A soft ivory pastel was used over red oxide. The angular nature of the male's body has been emphasized.

RIGHT In this charcoal drawing, the flat planes of the model's torso and limbs can clearly be seen.

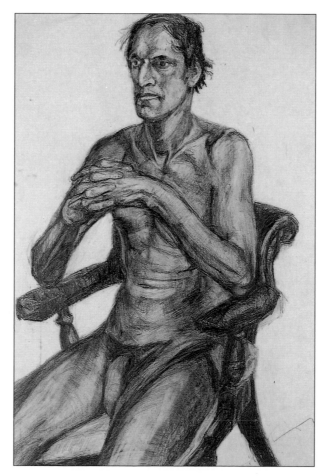

OPPOSITE A strong side light defines the forms of the body here. Shadows were blocked in with soft pastel.

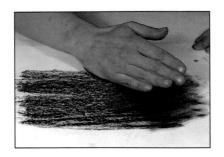

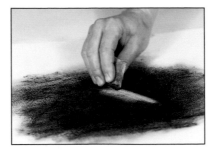

LEFT You can rub the charcoal with the flat side of the hand to blend it, then lift out any areas with a kneaded eraser. The eraser can also be used on the edge to draw lines into the charcoal.

Modeling the planes of the body with charcoal

Charcoal should be used on bond, charcoal, Ingres, or pastel paper. Papers with a smooth surface are not suitable.

There are many variations of modeling with charcoal, but they all begin with a simple sketch in charcoal pencil to place the figure. If you plan to draw the background of the room, you should indicate this in the drawing as well. It might be helpful to think of modeling as a process of subtraction by which we leave only the light that is on the figure and in the room. Some people like to think of putting in the shadows, but I prefer to try to see where the light is and to hold onto that as I work. Whichever method you choose, and your choice will also depend on the pose, your priority must be to determine the direction of the light and to keep it consistent throughout the drawing. You will find it easier to see the boundary on the body where the light changes to shadow if you use a small spotlight to begin with. When you have identified that edge, begin modeling with either the side of the charcoal stick or use small crosshatch lines to build up a tone. Try to draw the overall shape of the light and shadow, and remember that scattered, small areas of light or shadow tend to break up the form

and destroy the volume you are trying to create.

In general, it is best to leave the blending until last. Put in the modeling and leave it rough. When you have finished the drawing, you will be able to see the "whole" form and balance it by lightly rubbing or blending back certain areas. There are some modeling techniques in which a completely smooth effect is desired, and the drawing should then be blended from the outset.

Kneaded eraser has joined the traditional white chalk and pastel for highlighting. You can pick out the lights by rubbing or just pressing on an area, and many artists now "draw" with the eraser. Use the end of it as you would a pencil to make light lines, like crosshatching, on the figure or in the background in the charcoal tone.

Charcoal sticks will give a darker, richer black to a drawing. They are heavier than charcoal pencil and difficult to lift out or erase. Conte crayon can be used in the same way as charcoal, and burnt sienna and umber conte are also frequently used for warmer flesh tones. The medium has many possibilities which you will enjoy discovering. Remember that charcoal drawings must be sprayed with a fixative and, if possible, covered with a sheet of tracing paper to protect the surface when they are stored.

OPPOSITE ABOVE LEFT A charcoal drawing of a male nude with his weight on both feet. This is a strong composition, in which the stark lighting on the figure dominates. The artist's primary intention was to look for the relationship of shapes in the room and figure. The angles and planes of the body are counterbalanced by the curve of the drapery behind the figure. The heavy charcoal drawing was slightly blended to make a smoother surface before the light areas were further defined. Most of the light areas were lifted out with a kneaded eraser.

OPPOSITE ABOVE RIGHT The technique of this charcoal drawing contrasts with the illustration next to it. The original charcoal drawing has not been blended in the background and only slightly on the figure. The light areas have been lifted out. The artist has continued his search for the relationship of the shapes to the point where the profusion of shapes in the composition is assuming an abstract quality, and the figure is integrated as only one element of the totality.

OPPOSITE BELOW LEFT This nude male sitting on a stool is a classic example of modeling with charcoal. The planes of the body are defined with light charcoal modeling and crosshatching; the highlights are lifted with a kneaded eraser. Whether or not the model was sunburned, the artist's decision to draw the left arm as if it were tanned is useful in separating the form of the arm from the tone of the abdomen.

OPPOSITE BELOW RIGHT A charcoal drawing of a male nude holding a pole. This is a fine example of the way in which the planes of the body can be used to express the strength and virility of the male figure. The design is helped by darkening the negative space of the background and by using a cast shadow, which creates further depth in the picture plane.

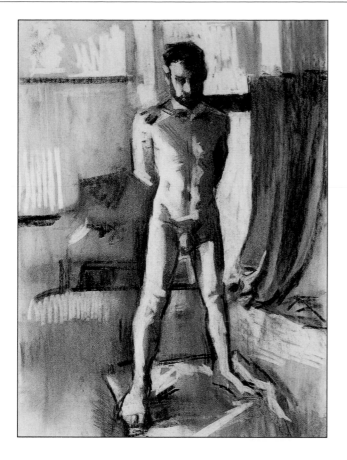

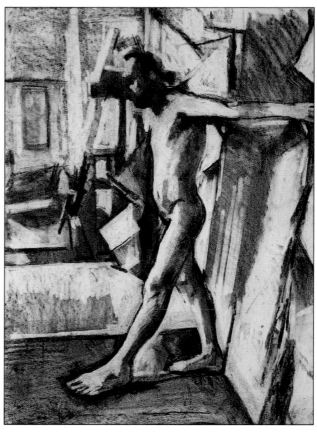

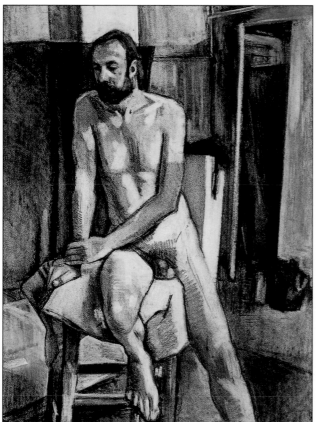

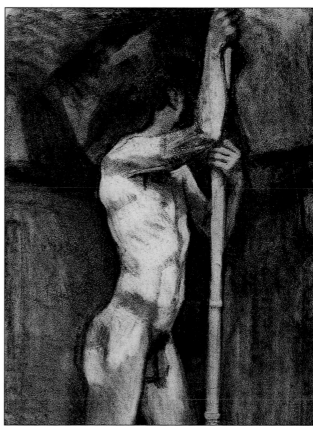

STAGES IN MODELING WITH CHARCOAL

V A N E S S A   W H I N N E Y

This is one of the basic techniques of modeling the form. The charcoal is used on both the end and side. A simple pose gives the best result. In this case the model is lying below the artist's eye level, and there is a profusion of tumbling curves through hips and legs which give the pose a quiet and relaxed mood.

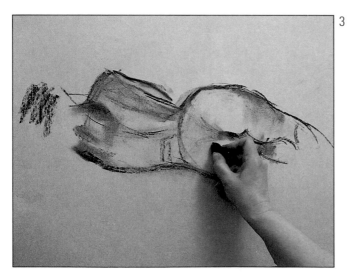

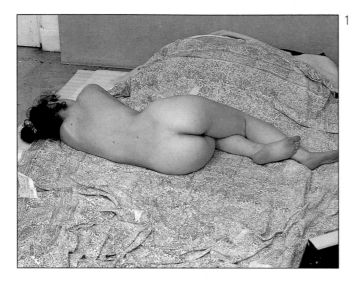

1 There is a flat light on the model. The artist will have to use a bit of imagination with the modeling to avoid an insipid drawing.

2 The basic curving movements are put in lightly. Since the key to the pose is in the back and hips, the artist has rightly started at this point.

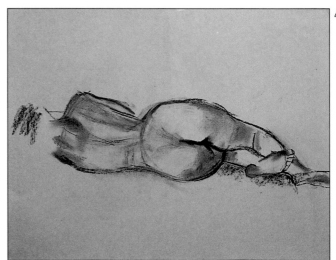

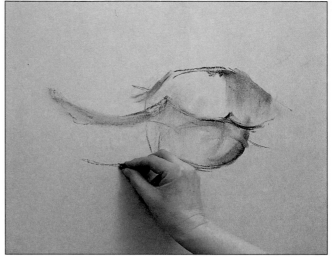

3 The side of the charcoal is being used to put in the broad planes on the figure.

4 The basic drawing is in place; the artist has worked across the entire figure without becoming involved with the details.

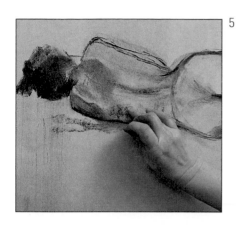

5

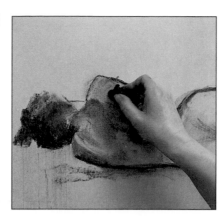

6

5 The rough charcoal is being lightly blended with the finger.

6 The tones and lines are being strengthened where needed.

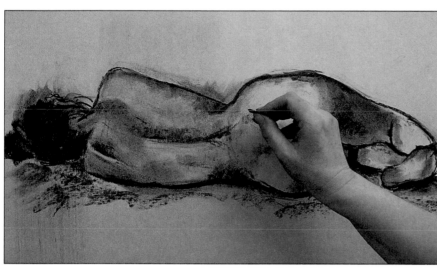

7

7 The sharp detail is being drawn in with charcoal pencil.

8 The model's weight and the softness of the flesh are beautifully rendered in this finished drawing.

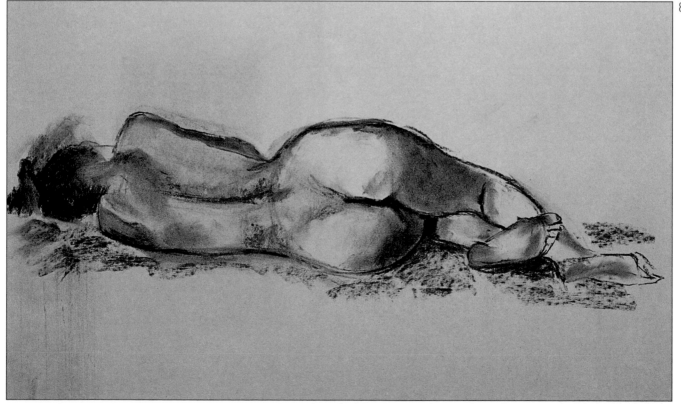

8

MODELING WITH PENCIL

Although what we see is not composed of line, some artists have been able to achieve a poetic illusion of reality using only a pencil. It is a mistake to believe that the pencil is simple to use – far from it. The pencil is the modern replacement for silverpoint, one of the most demanding and tedious media that artists have ever inflicted upon themselves. It involved drawing with silver wire on specially prepared paper. The silver left an indelible line of minute metal particles, which darkened as it tarnished. A pencil is superficially easier to use than silverpoint, but the inherent problems of the medium are still present: the quality of the line and its evenness, flow, and density must be controlled, but at the same time it must be lively, responsive, and above all, sensitive. The ideal is to communicate all with almost nothing.

The line was first used for drawing the contour of an object, but artists slowly developed ways to use it to create areas of tone as well. There are many ways in which a line can be used to make a tone. The traditional

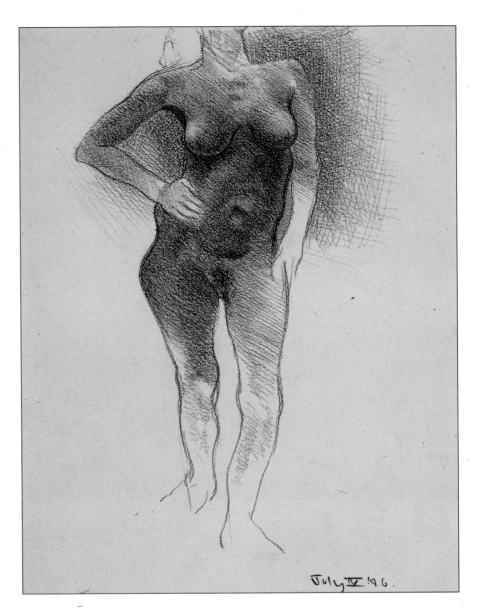

RIGHT ABOVE **The fine modelling of the standing female nude is drawn with a well-sharpened hard pencil, and the delicate lines almost merge into a solid grey tone. This is a difficult and laborious technique, which begins with a light contour drawing. The hatching lines are slowly built up, layer by layer, over the whole area to be modelled, and the details are drawn by the use of additional lines, which darken the specific area. The evenness and density of the lines give the drawing a sculptural quality that is difficult to obtain with a pencil.**

RIGHT **A beautiful drawing done with a conte pencil. Catching the relaxation of the body so precisely with the clear definition of the muscles took a great deal of patient concentration.**

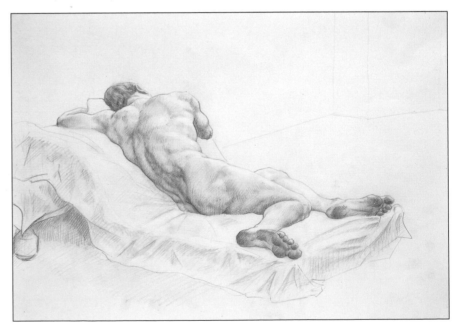

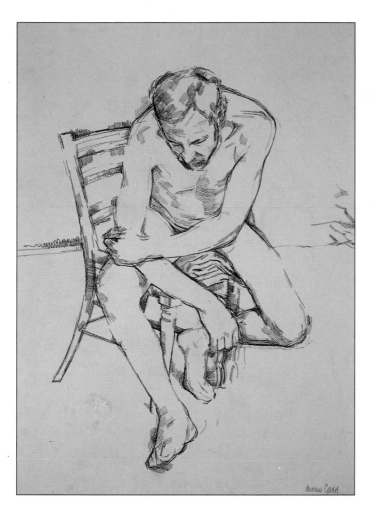

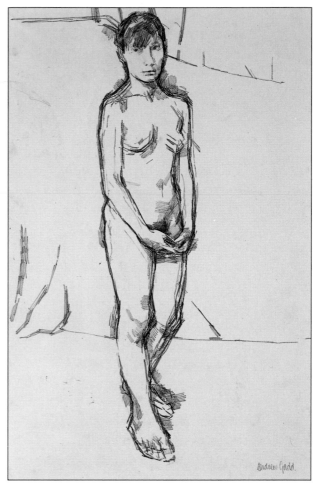

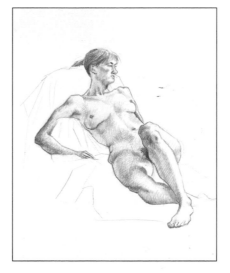

method is by hatching, when fine lines are drawn parallel to each other and close together. When you use a second layer of lines over the first, we call it crosshatching. Lines can also create tones with a random pattern, the so-called scribble lines. In both methods the tone is created and darkened by multiplying the number of lines and drawing them closer together. In modern drawings, both kinds of line are used and are frequently mixed.

The type of pencil you choose is critical to the type of drawing you plan. A hard pencil, HB to 4H, is suitable for fine work; a 6B or 8B will give a darker, broader line. The quality of the line is determined by the pressure you use on the pencil, and its point. For fine work the point of the pencil should be

sharpened on the finest sandpaper. If you want a broad, dark line, choose a soft pencil, such as 6B or 8B, and use a mat knife to cut the point, shaping the graphite to a chisel point for a wide or narrow line.

ABOVE LEFT AND RIGHT **These very subtle pencil drawings of a man seated on a chair and a woman standing are perfectly created three-dimensional forms with the minimum of pencil modeling. The artist has obviously studied the work of Paul Cézanne (1839–1906) who wrote: "Treat nature by the cylinder, the sphere, the cone, everything in proper perspective so that each side of an object or plane is directed toward a central point."**

LEFT **A drawing done with colored pencil. The crosshatchings used to model the forms are so fine they merge into a half-tone. The artist has caught the movement of the body from the twist of the outstretched foot up through the shoulder very well.**

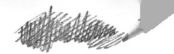

MODELING WITH COLORED PENCILS

J U S T I N   J O N E S

Using two colors for crosshatching gives this sketch additional depth and warmth. The lines move loosely, glancing off and then tucking around and behind the forms. The drawing has a lyrical quality enhanced by the merging of the red and blue lines into a pale violet hue.

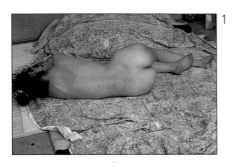

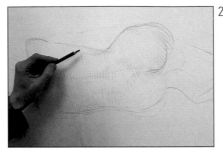

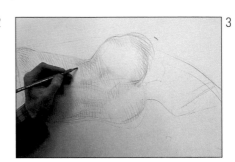

1 The model is lying below the artist's eye level.

2 The artist does a loose placement sketch of the entire body using the blue pencil.

3 The red pencil is used with the blue in the crosshatching.

4 The faint overall effect can now be seen.

5 As the artist adds more lines, the form slowly begins to emerge. This type of crosshatching work takes at least one or two hours to complete.

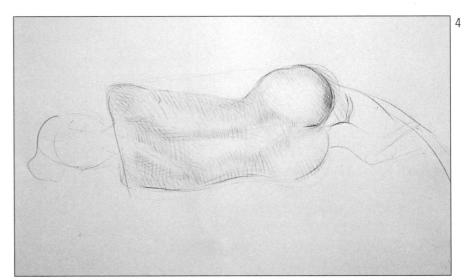

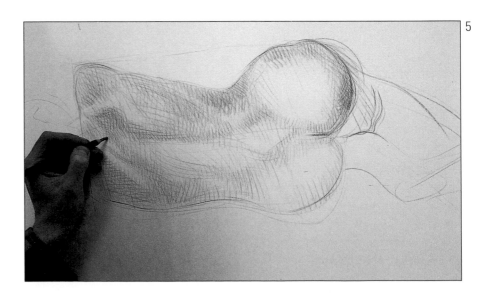

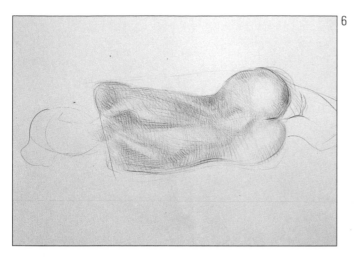

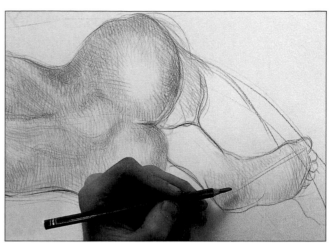

6 The drawing of the torso is now complete. The artist has concentrated on this area because it is the center of interest in the drawing.

7 The blue pencil is used for the darker tone to define the bottom plane of the foot.

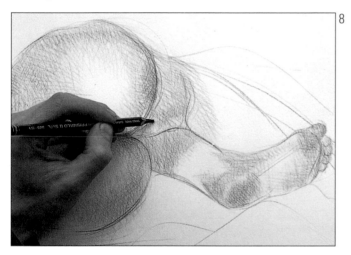

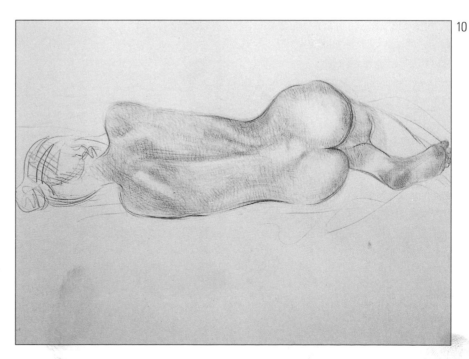

8 Using the blue pencil exclusively for the crosshatching will make the leg appear to go back in space.

9 The drawing is being "cleaned up" with a kneaded eraser.

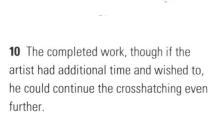

10 The completed work, though if the artist had additional time and wished to, he could continue the crosshatching even further.

CROSSHATCHING

J U S T I N · J O N E S

Crosshatching is one of the simplest ways to produce a gray tone. By gradually building up a web of fine lines, the artist has the time to consider carefully the subtle effect he is creating. He may go back to a drawing several times, slowly bringing out a part of the form by strengthening the hatching around it.

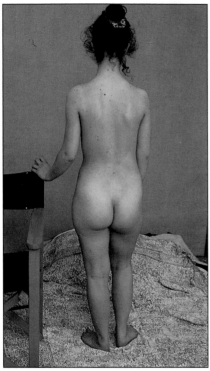

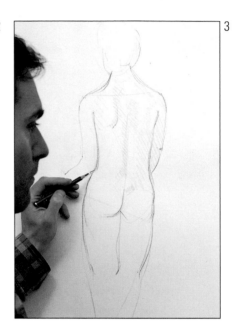

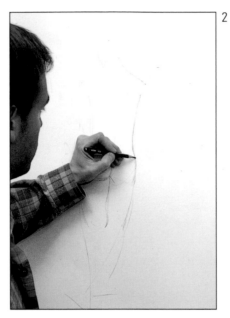

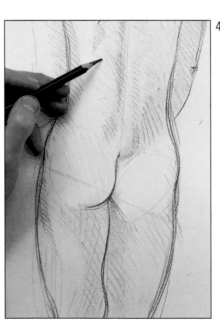

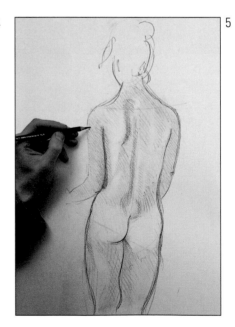

1 The model has assumed a simple pose which is ideal for crosshatching. Unfortunately, a standing pose cannot be held for a long time.

2 The artist begins with a contour drawing.

3 The most interesting part of the pose is the swing of movement through the back and hips, so the artist is concentrating on this portion of the figure.

4 In this detail you can see how the lines are drawn to enhance the roundness of the forms.

5 The artist works over the whole figure to complete the overall modeling.

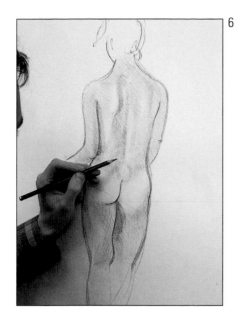

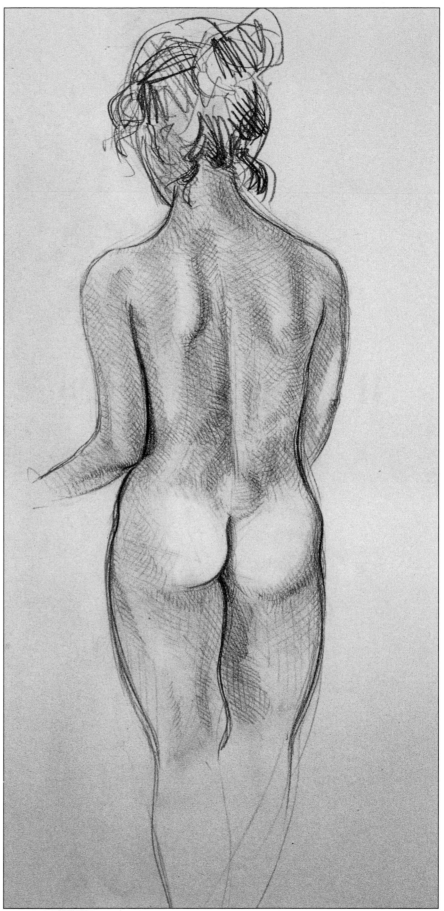

6 At this stage some of the details are being brought out by another layer of crosshatching.

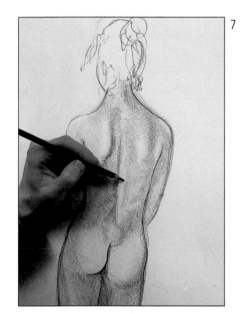

7 You can see how the tone deepens as each new layer of line is added.

8 The details of the hair have been added at this last stage. The looseness of the line the artist has used for the hair contrasts pleasingly with the controlled cross-hatching.

10
LINE DRAWINGS

Line drawing has a purity and simplicity. It looks quite easy, rather like watercolor painting, but do not be deceived; both techniques take skill and experience.

In a successful line drawing, a great deal must be implied and suggested without the aid of modeling, and the major problem is to create the illusion of space and volume. Trying to make a drawing appear three-dimensional with a line, which by its nature is one-dimensional, is an intellectual challenge.

One part of the solution is the use of perspective. Drawing the stand or chair on which the model is lying or sitting will help to define the space around her. If you plan a large composition, draw the background of the room to describe the depth of the picture plane. In a line drawing I would recommend that you slightly exaggerate the effects of fore-shortening on the figure. For example, if the model is sitting on a chair facing you, the depth from her knees to her back must be convincing if you are to create the illusion of three dimensions. In this case, the knees, shins, and feet would be proportionally larger because they are closer to you than the torso and head, which are further back in the chair. The more extreme the foreshortening of the figure, the greater the illusion of space.

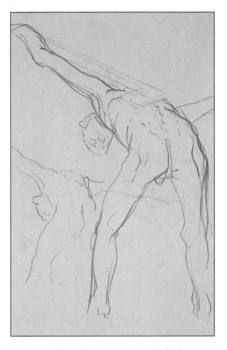

A B O V E By using as many straight lines as possible in this conte pencil drawing, the angular nature of the male figure has been emphasized. The head is drawn only lightly so that it will go back in space.

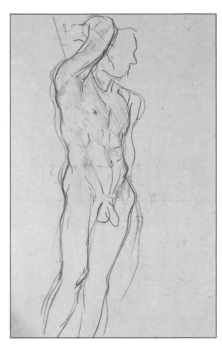

A B O V E In this conte pencil study, both the keen observation of the artist and the fluid quality of the line give this drawing its distinction. The line never hesitates; it flows down the figure.

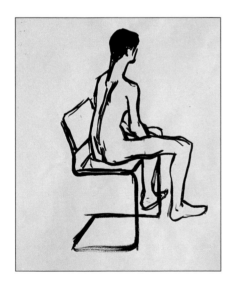

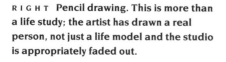

A B O V E This drawing was done with a Chinese brush, which was a good choice for drawing the thin, bony quality of the girl's body.

R I G H T Pencil drawing. This is more than a life study; the artist has drawn a real person, not just a life model and the studio is appropriately faded out.

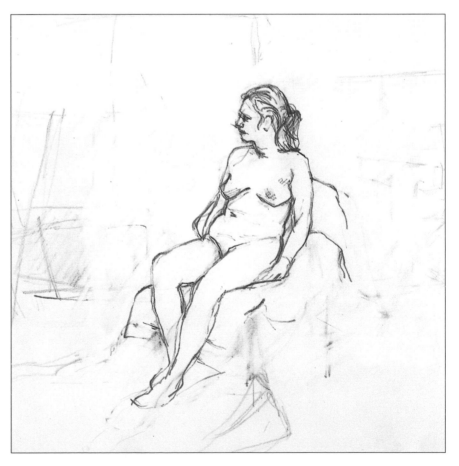

The second problem lies in suggesting the volume of the body. Your aim is to avoid drawing a figure that looks like a flat cutout, and to do this you must imagine the volume as you draw. Each limb has a three-dimensional form, and you should allow enough space for the round volume. For example, if a model is sitting with her legs or arms crossed and you draw the parts too close together, they will seem to be occupying the same space and almost to be "inside" each other.

There is an old trick that artists use to create a roundness in the form. Wherever one part of the body overlaps another, at a bend or joint, for example, the line of the form in front is emphasized to show it clearly crossing over the form behind it.

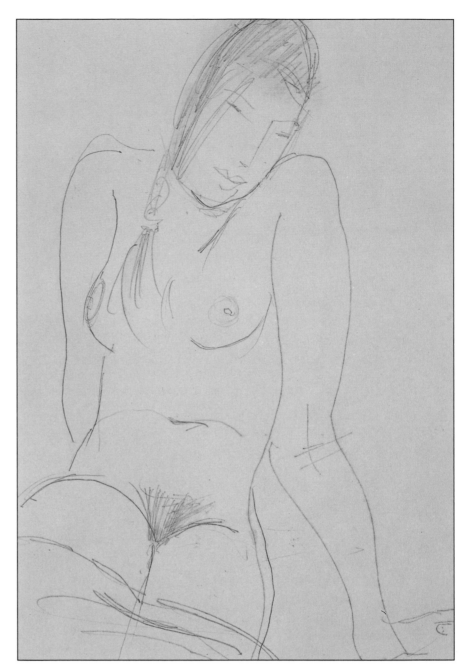

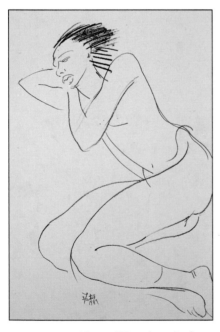

ABOVE **A rapid pencil line shows both movement and the volume of the figure. The heavy slashes of charcoal for the hair moves our eye to the sleeper's face.**

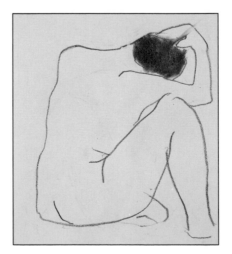

ABOVE **The artist has used a dry, light line to give this drawing a very different feel from his others on this page. The figure is beautifully composed to move over and fill the page.**

LEFT **A complete composition done in a few simple elegant lines. The tone of the hair is off-center, giving movement and balancing the drawing.**

BEGINNING A LINE DRAWING

No preliminary sketch is made with line drawings. The essence of the work is the free, loose quality of the line, and if you draw over a pencil line with a pen, it loses that freshness. If possible, the quality of the line should not belie the problems of the drawing. Although you will almost inevitably make mistakes, it is better to develop a confident line at the outset instead of being hesitant, which will break up the flow and grace, which constitute the "poetry" of the line. Paul Klee (1879–1940) described his drawings "as taking a line for a walk," and this is a valid comparison,

for as it travels along the form, the line describes the shape.

There is a good selection of pencils and pens to use for line drawings, and they make a great variety of distinctive lines. It is useful to practice with them before you start your drawing so that you develop a feel for what they can do.

You can choose between the smooth line of a pencil and the jagged, dry mark of a bamboo pen. I prefer to use a soft pencil for larger line drawings, because I find the line of a hard pencil is too light on its own. Felt-tip pens are now often used for line drawings, but although they are convenient and quick,

unfortunately very few have permanent inks. Before you buy, ask if the colors are fugitive or permanent. Colored pencils and pastel pencils are very interesting to use, and they give you the opportunity to use more than one color in a drawing. There are also various kinds of drawing pen that have an ink cartridge, which makes them very useful.

The paper you use will also make a difference to the drawing. The smoother the paper, the sharper the line will be. You will find that a textured paper, such as a light watercolor paper, is better for a bamboo pen.

DRAWING THE NUDE WITH LINE

JUSTIN JONES

The drawing has been done with a stick of hard blue pastel. The artist has to sharpen the stick with a craft knife or sandpaper block from time to time, to keep the line from thickening. The quality of the line is of paramount importance if the drawing is to succeed.

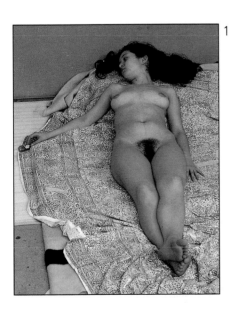

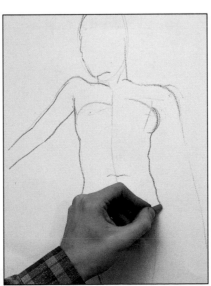

1 The model is posing below eye level.

2 The artist is drawing directly, without the aid of guidelines, to keep the flow of the line.

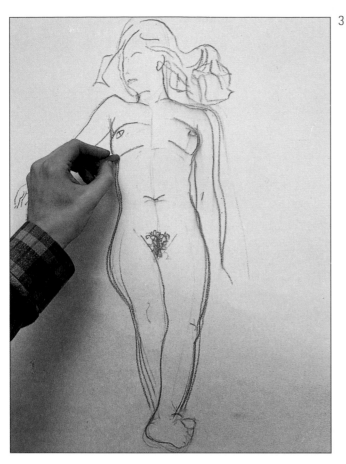

3

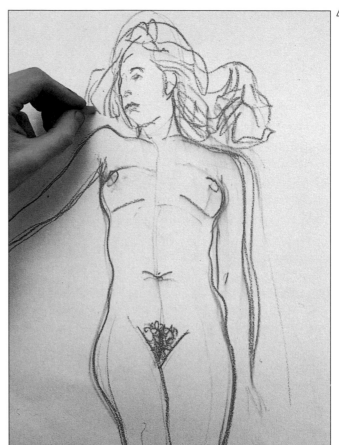

4

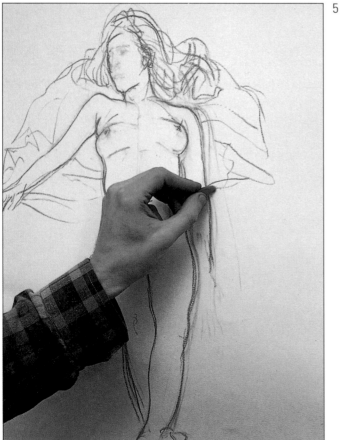

5

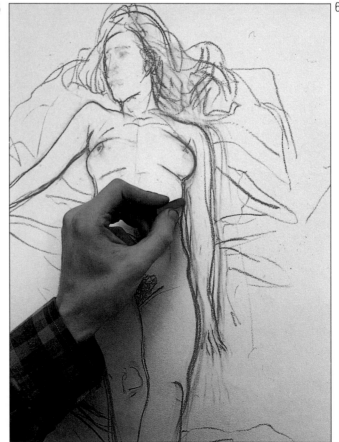

6

3 The basic contours of the figure have been drawn, and the long, curving lines of the body have not been interrupted by unnecessary detail.

4 This detail shows how the artist has created volume by drawing the breasts on the curve of the rib cage.

5 The artist draws the soft pillow and cloth under the model's head to give the sense of weight to her body.

6 Here the artist begins to strengthen some of the lines and correct the position of the model's left arm.

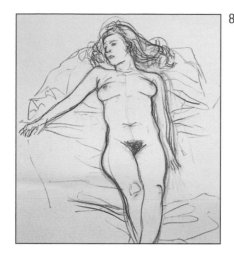
8

8 The drawing seems complete. However, there is a problem. The top half of the figure is not lying back sufficiently.

9 The artist blurs the details of the face and smudges a shadow across the upper chest to make it appear to recede. Now the drawing works well.

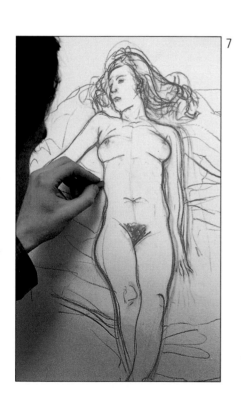
7

7 Here the details of the head have been drawn in.

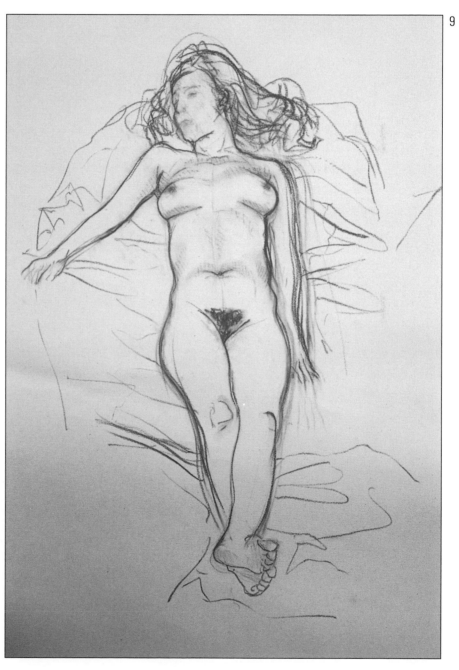
9

11

PASTEL TECHNIQUES

Pastels are both a drawing and a painting medium, forming a perfect bridge between the two. Quick and versatile to use, they are made of pure artists' pigments, which give both brilliance and subtlety. It is perhaps significant that Degas, a superb draftsman, chose pastel for much of his innovatory work in color and composition. Pastel colors on acid-free paper will remain permanent if the work is protected by framing or careful storage.

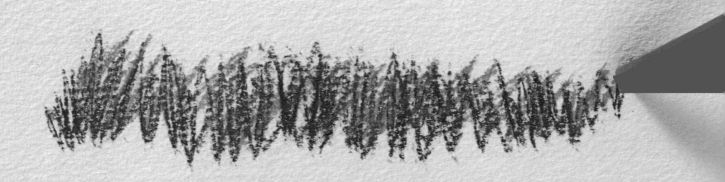

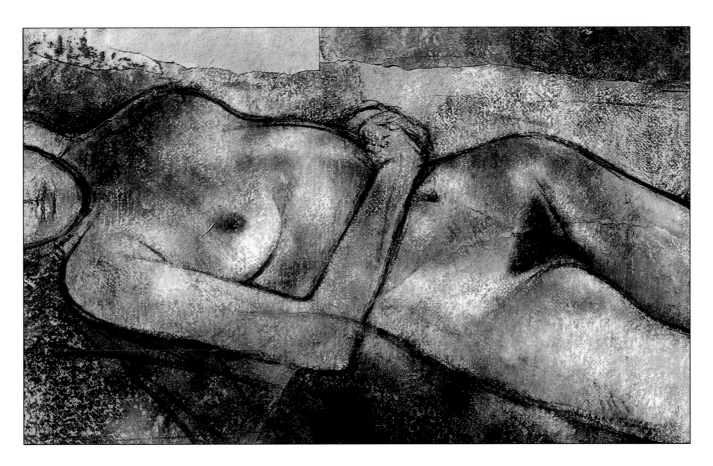

Pastels enable you to draw with color, building up or changing a composition quickly without having to wait for the paint to dry. The textures that are possible with pastels are completely unique to the medium. A rough watercolor paper will give you a heavily textured drawing that can still be blended smooth in areas for contrast. Tinted papers with fairly neutral colors can provide you with a medium shade that will "hold" the picture together as you compose the light and dark areas.

The type of paper you select is important. A slick or smooth paper does not have enough "tooth" to hold the pastel, and bond paper is suitable only for quick drawings. The surface texture of the paper must be protected and maintained, and not allowed to collapse or flatten, for if it does, the paper will soon become impossible to work on. To stop this

ABOVE *The Kitaj Girl, Lynne.* **R.B. Kitaj (b. 1932) is one of the foremost contemporary artists using pastel today, and the artist Justin Jones has used a technique similar to one of Kitaj's for this study. The side of the charcoal was used to produce the loose, dark tone on beige paper, and light alizarin and yellow ocher pastels were gently worked into the charcoal and the light areas. The line drawing was done with charcoal pencil. As the drawing developed, darker shades were put under and around the figure to bring it out. The lovely grays in the shadows are the result of the pastel and charcoal mixing on the beige paper. White pastel was later added for the highlights and background.**

hardening of the surface, use fresh bread to make any erasures. The slight dampness in the bread absorbs the pigment without pushing it into the paper. A normal eraser will smear the pastel into the surface and flatten the texture of the paper, so that with each correction further work on the drawing becomes increasingly difficult. I try to avoid making any erasure if possible, preferring to draw over the part I want to change. Pastel covers well, and I think that the gradual, probing build-up of lines is interesting and does not detract from the work. If it is possible to see where Degas moved a hand or limb in his work, why should we be embarrassed to show our revisions?

There are several ways to use pastel, and one of the pleasures of this versatile medium is the freedom it offers to experiment with new ideas.

PASTEL TECHNIQUES

Pastel is a very popular medium. The colors themselves are beautiful, and they can be used in a great variety of ways. As you work, the pastels almost seem to suggest new ideas to you. Drawings can be built up or changed in a few minutes. Here are just a few of the many techniques you may wish to try.

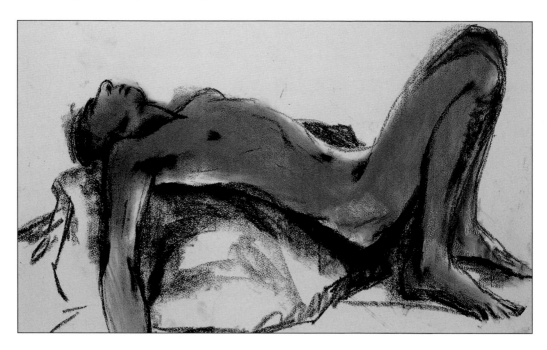

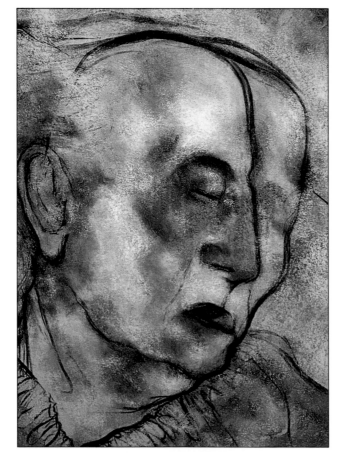

ABOVE Only two colors were used for this quick sketch: the black line is soft pastel, not charcoal. The placement of the figure was made by using a conte on its side, then rubbing it, and the drawing was added after the mass was blocked in.

LEFT *Lillian*. In this drawing the white paper has been lightly rubbed with charcoal to give it a texture, and the drawing of the head has also been done with charcoal. The pastel color is kept to a minimum to produce this sensitive portrait of an old friend.

OPPOSITE Soft pastel on dark gray paper. Using dark paper as a background has the advantage that the light colors and flesh tones stand out easily against it. This artist has used the paper well, creating both a life study and a striking portrait.

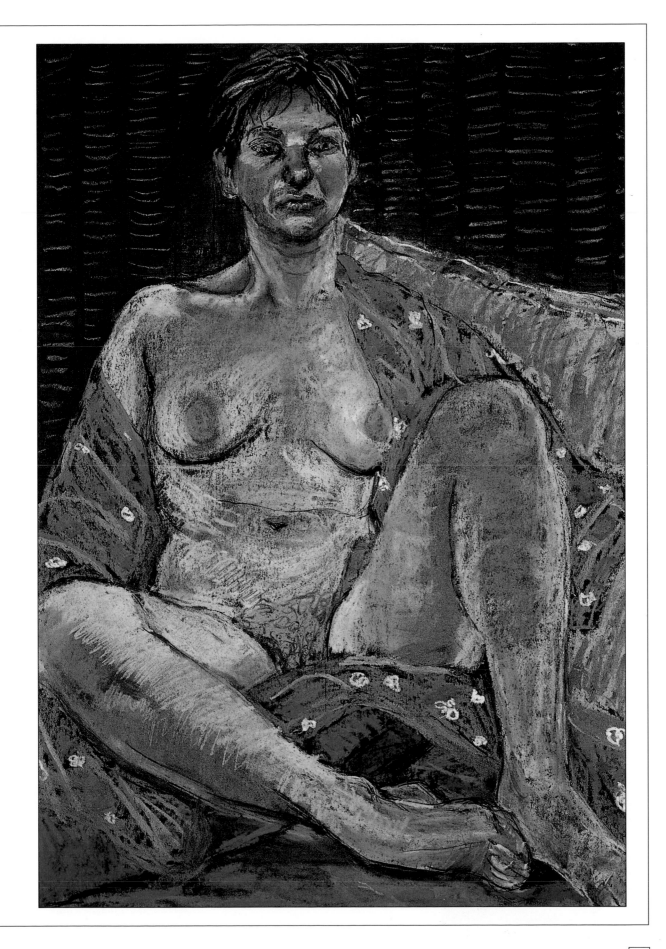

USING PASTEL

A pastel stick can be used to make a great variety of marks, depending on the way you hold the stick and how much pressure you exert. If you hold the stick at the end, you make a line; you can use it at a sharp angle to the paper and flat to produce a variable tone. The more you press, the deeper the shade becomes. You can mix the colors on the paper by lightly layering one color on top of another. If you do not want the colors to mix, use a fixative spray between layers. The color can be blended together with a blending stick for very fine detail. You can also use the driest part of your hand, which is the edge of the flat side or the little finger, or a clean dry tissue.

I usually do the blending at the end and use it sparingly. I prefer a looser style of drawing, and blending tends to tighten the work. However, it is very much a question of individual taste and, of course, depends on the subject matter.

For quick sketching you might try rubbing the paper with scene painters' charcoal, or if this is unobtainable, a thick stick of normal charcoal. Once you have applied this loose coat, you can draw onto it with charcoal or pastel. When the pastel is used on its side, it will mix slightly with the charcoal to create a subtle color and shading.

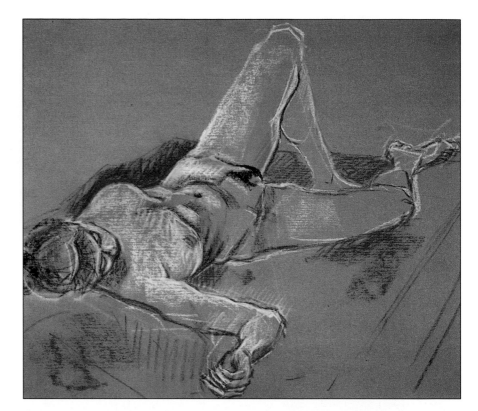

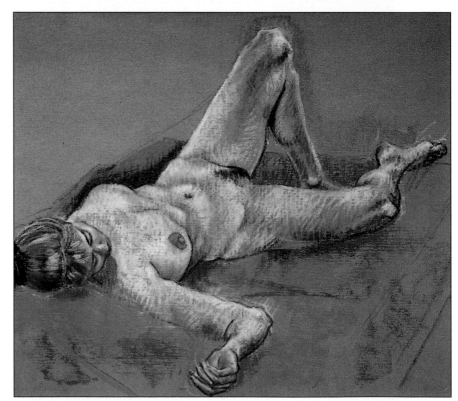

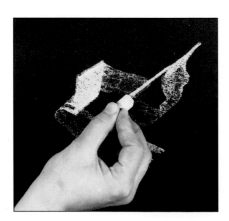

LEFT **This demonstration shows how the shade and color of the pastel changes with the amount of pressure you use.**

ABOVE **Pastel has been used on abrasive paper here, which means that the pastel is held firmly in the paper. It cannot be blended, but the colors can be layered very easily to produce a drawing that resembles a painting.**

USING HARD PASTEL ON TINTED PAPER

VIVIEN TORR

Hard pastel is closer to conte sticks than to soft pastel. It is generally used on the sharpened tip like a colored pencil. It is possible to build up the forms and colors by crosshatching lines, as this graceful drawing demonstrates.

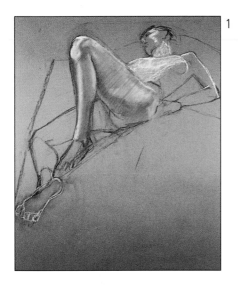

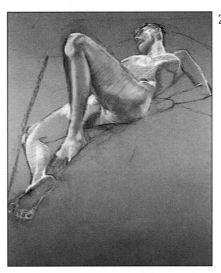

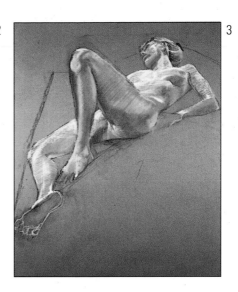

1 The basic drawing is done with the neutral pastel on tinted paper, and the light shades are added first.

2 The artist has begun crosshatching warm flesh tones into the light areas of the figure.

3 The figure slowly emerges with the warm colors and appears almost three-dimensional on the page.

4 The completed drawing. The sharp edges and lines of the hard pastel give this drawing a more graphic quality than could be achieved with a soft pastel. Hard pastel can be used on its side, but it tends to flatten the surface of a fine paper very quickly.

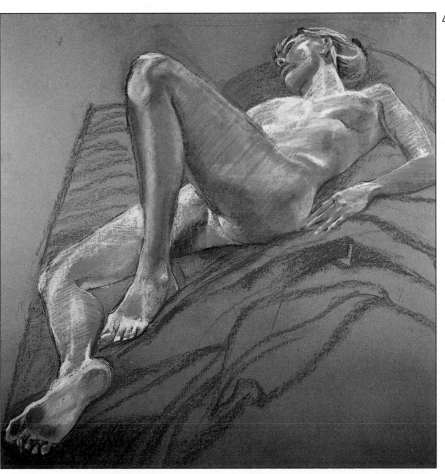

DRAWING WITH TWO SHADES OF PASTEL

DIANA CONSTANCE

Sometimes by limiting the number of colors you use, a more striking effect can be achieved. This drawing is a monochrome in which two shades of yellow ocher have been used. The desired effect was to create the sketch just by drawing the shadows and light on the body without using a line.

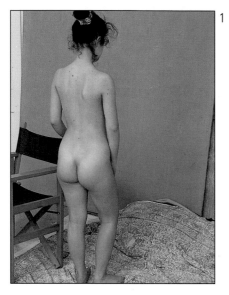

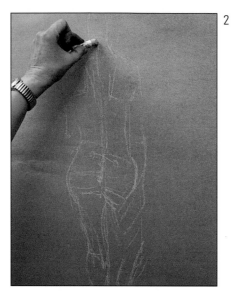

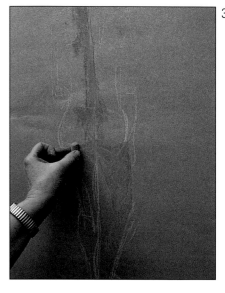

1 The model has assumed a standing pose with most of her weight on the left leg. For this long standing pose, the model was given a chair to hold on to.

2 A simple drawing is completed first using a neutral gray pastel on the tinted paper which has been selected.

3 With a darker shade, the shadow areas are drawn in, starting with the twist of the spine.

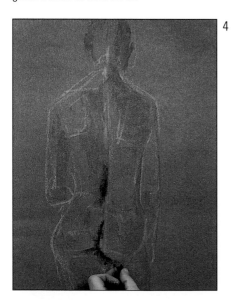

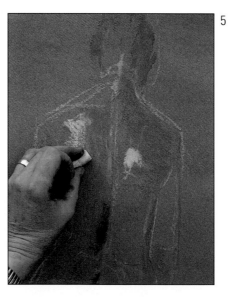

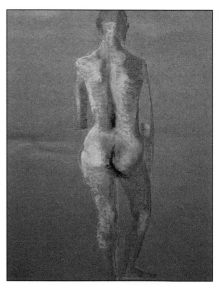

4 The shadow areas are complete, and the darkest shade is added to emphasize the movement through spine and hips.

5 Using a very soft pastel, barely touching the surface of the paper, the light shades on the form start to be worked.

6 The basic pattern of light and shadow is established all over the body.

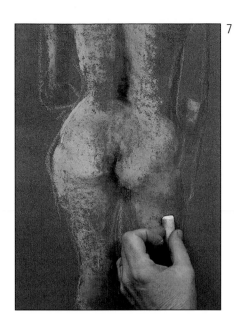

7

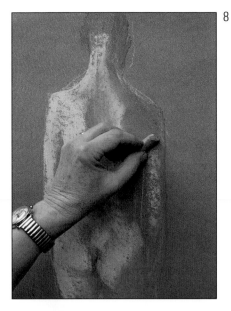

8

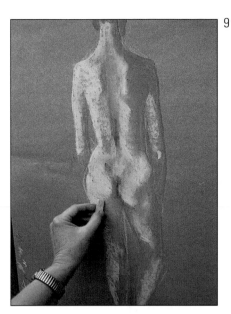

9

7 A detail showing how the light pastel is worked on top of and into the darker shade. They are being allowed to blend slightly, using fingers to rub them together.

8 Here the artist is sharpening up the shades and defining the planes of the body more clearly.

9 The final touches to the modeling are added to balance out the figure.

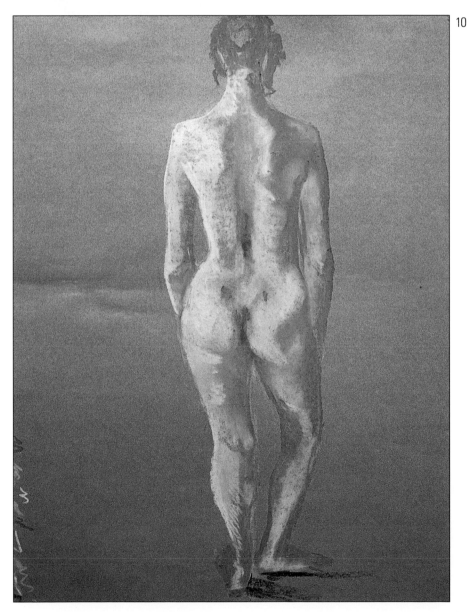

10

10 The completed sketch. You can see how the balance of the figure falls from the back of her neck to a point directly between her two feet. The chair has been omitted because it would have destroyed the simplicity of the drawing. You can now see how the figure rises from the paper, using nothing more than two shades of pastel.

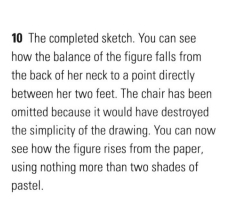

LAYERING PASTEL

For layering, you will need soft pastels and charcoal pencil and some watercolor paper.

For a large composition use charcoal pencil for the basic drawing of the figure and the overall composition. Use the same thin sticks to put in light crosshatching in all the areas that are in shadow. This method will mean that the tonal structure of the composition is planned before the color is added. It is particularly important with pastels to have a clear plan of the light and dark areas of the composition at the first stage of any work. Pastel colors are light and seductive, and it is quite easy to lose the bass notes and be left with a shallow piece that lacks structure.

Next, select a few colors and, with the flat side of the pastel, loosely put in the basic blocks of color that you plan to use. Repeat the colors in small areas in different parts of the drawing to "tie" it together. You will find that pastel mixes well with charcoal. A light blue or cool green in the shadows will mix with the charcoal and make a subtle blend.

Now that you have the basic structure, you can work into the drawing by loose hatching in color or by using the side of the pastel to continue to build the volume of the forms. Allow plenty of time and keep building up a tapestry of color that allows the layers underneath to show through. Avoid fixing until the drawing is finished.

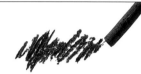

USING CHARCOAL WITH PASTEL

D I A N A   C O N S T A N C E

Charcoal and pastel are both dry-stick media and, as such, work well together. Charcoal is frequently used for the preliminary sketch. In this case, the artist has extended the idea and used it as a base tone for the drawing.

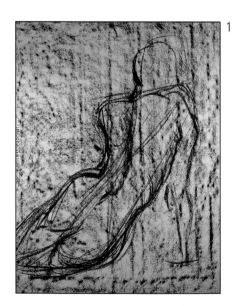

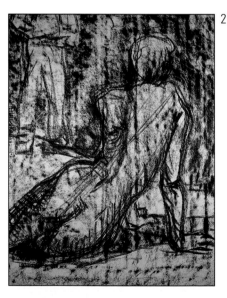

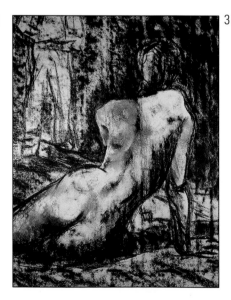

1 The paper has been rubbed with a block of soft charcoal and a quick sketch is made. Charcoal sticks are too heavy for this work.

2 A composition begins to emerge. The diagonal line leads the eye to the second figure.

3 The first very soft pastel is gently layered over the charcoal. Hard pastel would push away or mix with the charcoal underneath.

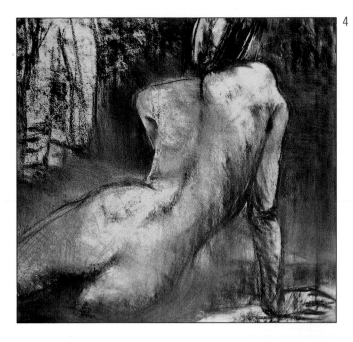

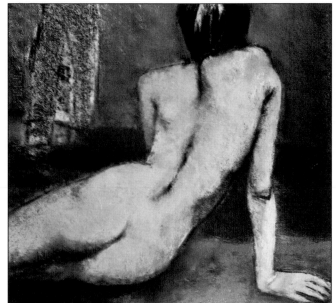

4 More pastel is added, and the shadows take on a silvery color as pastel and charcoal merge.

5 With the charcoal providing a dark base, note that the pastel color can become richer.

6 The finished work.

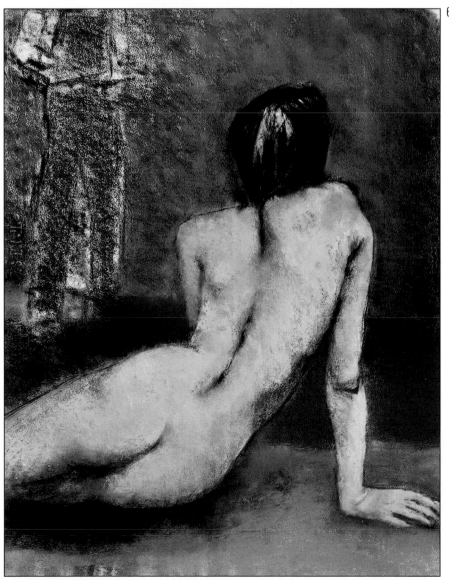

12

DRAWING THE HEAD

Drawing the head of a nude and the study of portraiture both begin with an understanding of the balance and movement of the complete figure. Every segment or part of the body we are drawing is a reflection of the whole person, and this is particularly the case with the head.

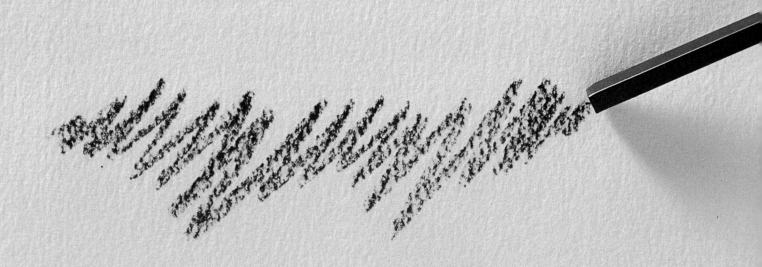

The head has a great deal of mobility. It rests like a globe on the atlas vertebra at the top of the cervical vertebrae of the upper spine. This beautifully designed bone allows the head to rotate easily back and forth and from side to side. It is one of the most flexible joints in the body. A great many muscles are required to hold the head in position, but the most obvious and important to the artist are the two sternomastoid muscles, which are connected just behind the ears. They wrap around the sides of the neck and join onto the breastbone and the clavicle or collarbone at the front. These are powerful muscles and are clearly visible in both men and women. They are used for turning the head, and they give a graceful curve or diagonal line to the neck, which it is important to express in the drawing.

The neck and head should always be seen and drawn together as a unit. Find and follow the direction of movement up through the spine and shoulders. I always start a drawing by looking at the whole pose to find the balance and movement. I note the position of the shoulders, then come up through the neck to find the right angle for the perch of the head.

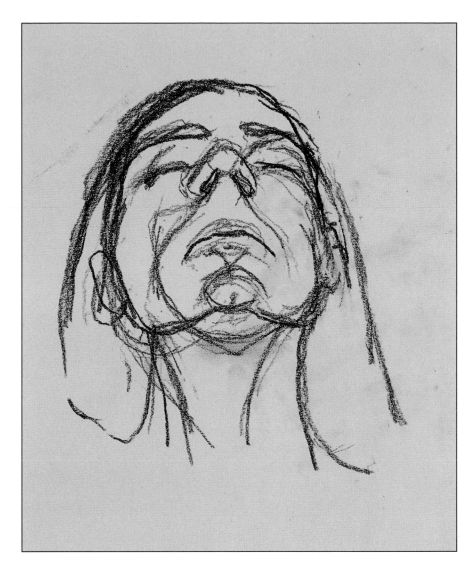

BELOW LEFT This drawing shows some of the bones of the skull and how they affect the outer structure of the face.

BELOW RIGHT The average skull is as deep, front to back, as the length of the face.

ABOVE In this sensitive pencil sketch of the head, note how the features wrap over and around the curve of the face.

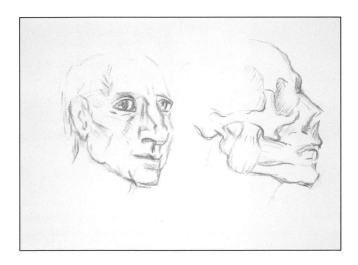

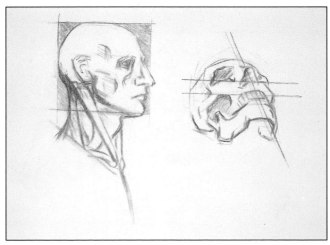

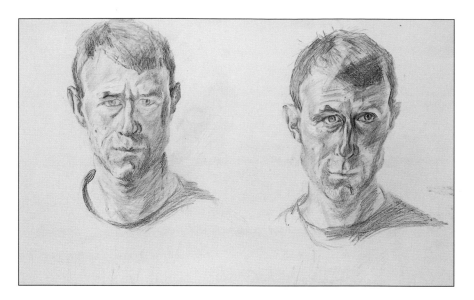

The cranium or skull is, on average, as deep as the face is long. The jaw is connected by ligaments to the upper part of the skull, which is important to remember when a model is resting her head on her hand. The entire lower part of the face will be pushed out of alignment by the thrust of weight on the hand and arm. If you draw this displacement correctly, you will give a convincing feeling of the weight of the head.

As long as the model's head is straight and at your eye level, it is quite easy to draw. Unfortunately, it is seldom held in this manner. So before you start to draw, consider three points. First, is the head under, above, or level with your eye level? Second, which way is the head tilting? Because the head is heavy, the angle of the tilt is bound to increase with time. Take this into account and allow a few minutes for the model to settle into the pose. Third, how much of the face are you seeing – full front, profile, or more likely, somewhere between the two?

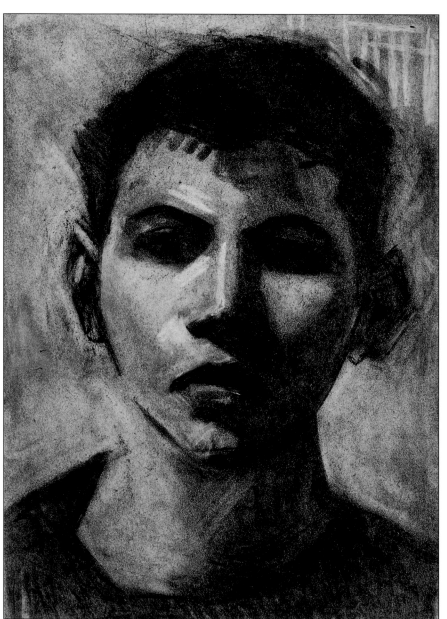

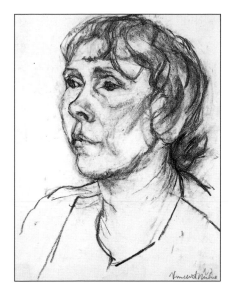

ABOVE Charcoal sketch in which you can see how well the artist has observed the curves of the woman's face.

RIGHT A self-portrait of the artist. Justin Jones used very fine hatching lines to build up the tonal structure, and the addition of more and more of these delicate lines, close together, gives this drawing a beautifully even, rounded form.

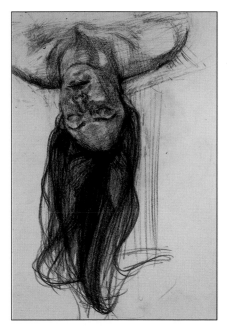

ABOVE The model must have been a good friend of the artist to take this lovely, but excruciatingly painful pose. There is a beautiful use of fluid line in both the hair and the crosshatching. The roundness of the forehead in particular is very convincing. The hair is drawn falling in a wave from the back of the head as well as the front, thus creating the three-dimensional quality of the drawing.

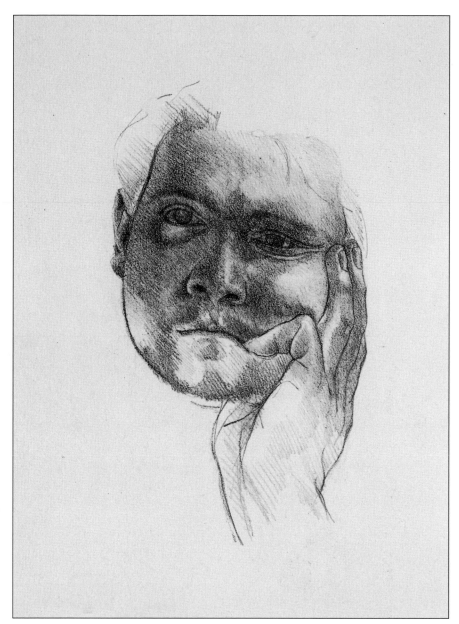

If you have a three-quarter view, determine exactly where the line of the middle of the face is and how much is foreshortened on the far side. The slightest change in position by yourself or the model will change this angle, so try to mark the position on the sheet with guidelines and hold to it, making any small adjustments by moving yourself as the model drifts out of the original alignment.

Once you have determined the position of the head, the next step is to draw a line for the middle of the face and light guidlines to place the features. The lines should wrap around the curved surface of the face or head and be parallel to each other. The ears of the average person line up with the top of the eye socket and the bottom of the nose. The angle or slant of the ear follows the line of the jaw, which it is behind. If you are interested in achieving a likeness, measure the triangles formed by the eyes and the bottom of the nose, mouth, and chin. This will give you the shape of that particular face.

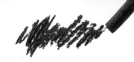

THE HEAD IN A FORESHORTENED POSE

D I A N A   C O N S T A N C E

There are two important things to remember about the head. First, we seldom hold our head straight since the head is heavy and is connected to the spinal column by the atlas vertebrae which, as their name implies, allow the head to move easily in almost any direction. The second point is that no single plane in the head is flat, particularly the curving surface of the face. The head is an elusive form to capture accurately.

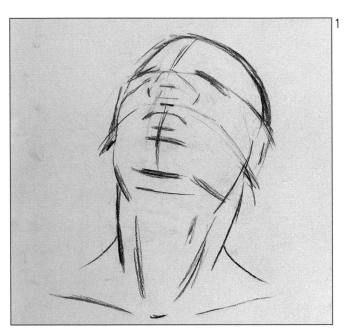

1

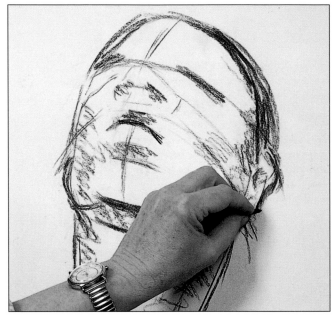

2

1 The head is begun with a light sketch, placing guidelines around the head so that you can position the features on the curving surfaces. Always draw an imaginary line going down the middle of the face to line up the features.

2 The modeling and details of the features are added gradually, following the guidelines.

3 The drawing is completed and you can see how the size of the chin, which is close to the viewer, is larger than the forehead which diminishes as it goes back. The two mastoid muscles are shown as they wrap around the neck from behind the ear and join up at the clavicle.

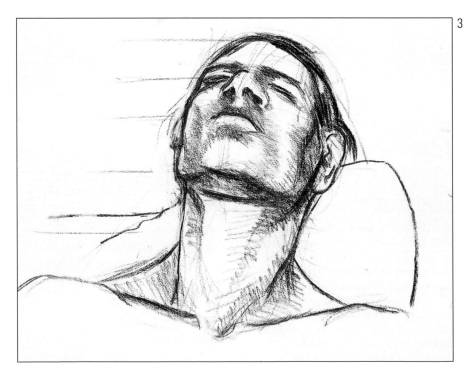

3

13

DRAWING HANDS AND FEET

The structure of both the hands and feet is complex, and it is worth giving extra time and effort to studying them. They are often daunting for the beginner, but the key to drawing them lies with understanding their basic structure. Studying a skeleton to see how the bones are joined will help.

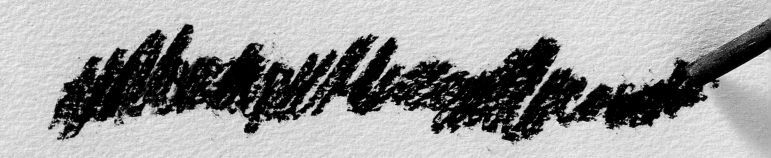

THE HANDS

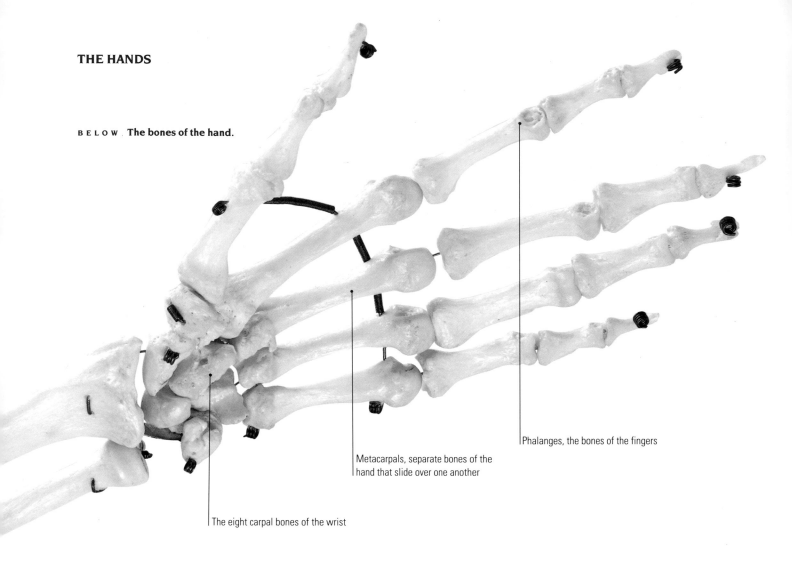

Phalanges, the bones of the fingers

Metacarpals, separate bones of the hand that slide over one another

The eight carpal bones of the wrist

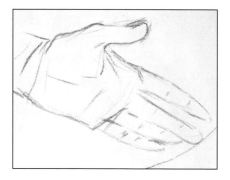

A B O V E **Conte drawing of the hand with a guideline to show the direction of the fingers.**

From the skeleton we can see that the hand is fan-shaped, its bones radiating out from the bones of the wrists. Each finger has four bones – the phalanges – and the thumb has three. The first bones, the metacarpals, are enclosed within the palm or main body of the hand, and the first joints of those bones are our knuckles. It is important to remember that the finger bones actually start at the wrist. Often the hand is drawn as a stiff block, with only the fingers gripping or moving. This movement should, in fact, be one piece, with the whole hand bending or curving in line with the fingers. The palm or top of the hand is very seldom straight or flat. When the arm and hand are relaxed and hanging freely, you can see a long, curving line running through the wrist down to the tips of the fingers. The thumb also curls around and rests facing the palm.

I always urge students to draw their own hands whenever they have a spare moment.

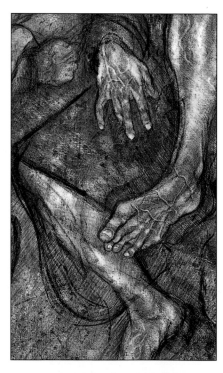

A B O V E **Pastel drawing. A detail from *Two Asian Women with Child* by Justin Jones.**

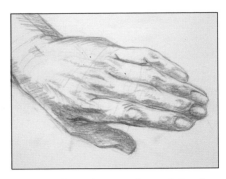

A B O V E Conte drawing of a man's hand.

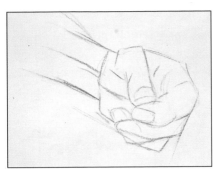

A B O V E The position of the forms are drawn first without the details.

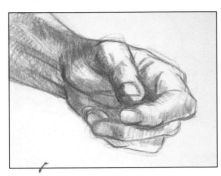

A B O V E The completed conte drawing with fine crosshatching lines to model the forms.

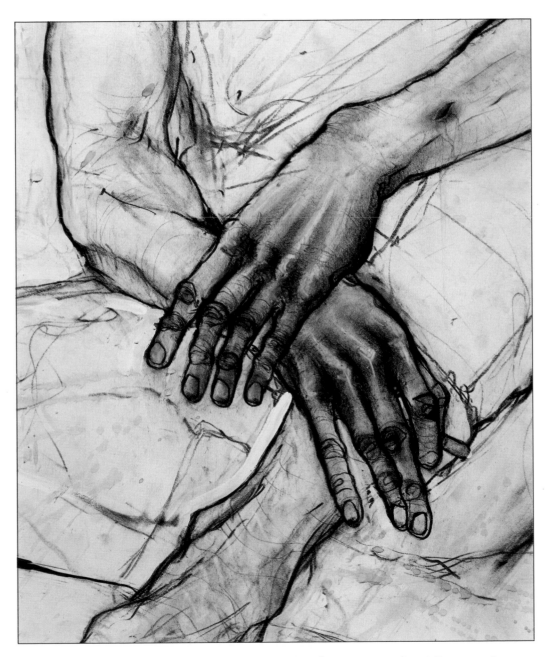

A B O V E Charcoal and pastel. The artist has studied the drawings of the German master Lucas Cranach (1472–1553), whose influence can be seen in the strong, clearly articulated hands.

THE MOVEMENT OF THE HANDS

As we draw, the tendency is to think that the movement of our hands is almost confined to the fingers. As we can see from the bones of the hand, the fingers are just extensions of the bones running through the so-called "flat" of our hand. When we move our fingers, the entire form of the hand changes, not just the fingers. These drawings help to demonstrate this point.

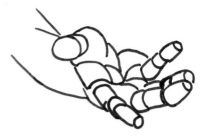

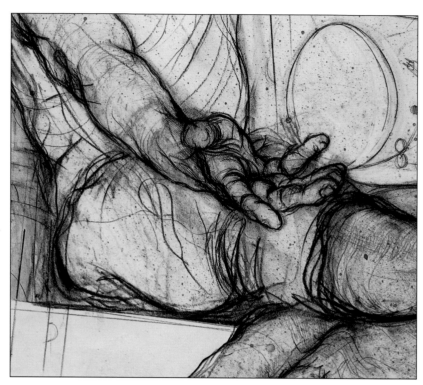

RIGHT AND ABOVE A charcoal drawing showing the way in which the palm of the hand and fingers curve around, almost forming a circle. This can be seen clearly in the simplified line drawing above.

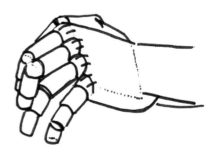

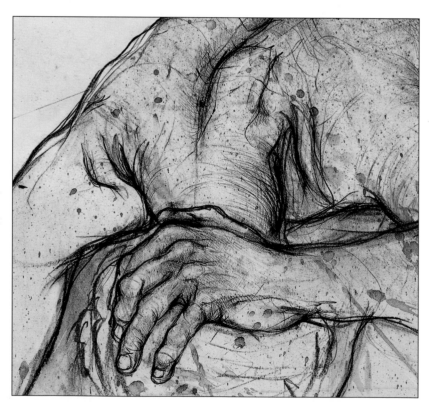

RIGHT AND ABOVE Charcoal drawing. The flexibility of the whole hand is clearly drawn, with the fan of the fingers stretching out to cover the back of the cranium.

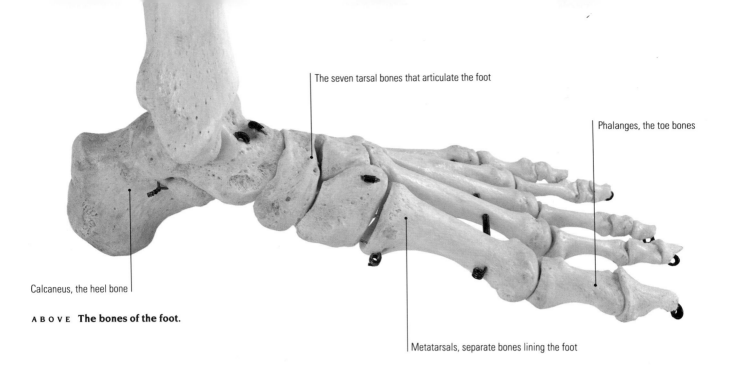

The seven tarsal bones that articulate the foot

Phalanges, the toe bones

Calcaneus, the heel bone

ABOVE **The bones of the foot.**

Metatarsals, separate bones lining the foot

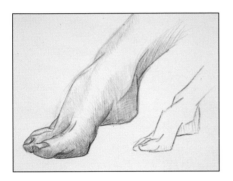

THE FEET

The foot is at least one head in length. As we have seen, the ankle joint permits movement freely forward and backward, with a limited rotation in the joint. The foot and the ankle are not symmetrical. From the front, the foot resembles an uneven triangle with the top cut off, sloping down on its outer side. The curve of the arch is visible only on the inner side of the foot. Put a wet foot on a piece of brown paper to form a footprint, and you will clearly see the flat outer edge, the arch, and the curve of the toes. From the skeleton you can see how much the heel bone protrudes from the back, but what is not visible in the skeleton is the strong Achilles' tendon, which connects to the top of the calcaneus or heel bone.

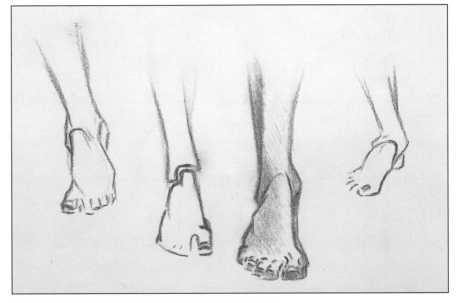

The ankle is formed by the ends of the tibia, the large shin bone, and the delicate fibula. These bones straddle the top of the foot and form the hinge joint. The large bulge on the inner ankle is the side of the tibia; it is higher than the fibula on the outer side. A good way to remember is that the lower ankle bone is on the sloping, outer side of the foot.

Drawing your own foot with the help of a long mirror is good practice and will save a lot of expensive model fees.

ABOVE LEFT **A conte drawing of the foot clearly showing the shape of the arch.**

ABOVE RIGHT **Conte drawings of the ankle joint. The bones of the lower leg, the tibia and fibula, tightly straddle the top of the foot. The inner bone of the ankle is higher than the outer.**

THE INDIVIDUALITY OF A FOOT

The feet can be as expressive as the hands. The old worn foot tells us a great deal about the person and the life they have led. Here are some very interesting feet displaying a multitude of different characteristics.

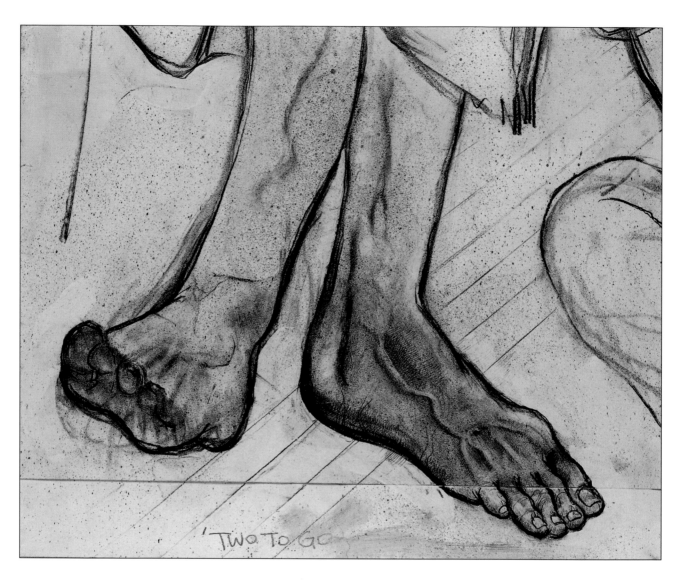

'Two To Go'

ABOVE An interesting charcoal and pastel drawing. The artist has observed not only the structure but also the individuality of the old feet, the metatarsal joints twisted from years of ill-fitting shoes.

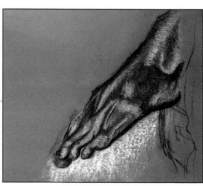

LEFT A charcoal drawing on red paper, highlighted with white chalk. This carefully modeled drawing took the student two hours of hard work. It is important not to rush yourself when you work on this type of study.

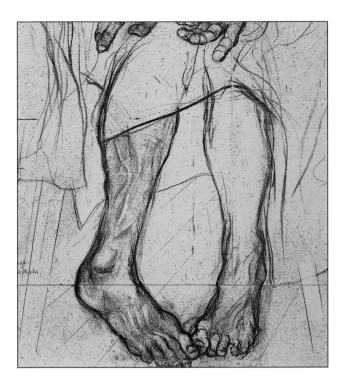

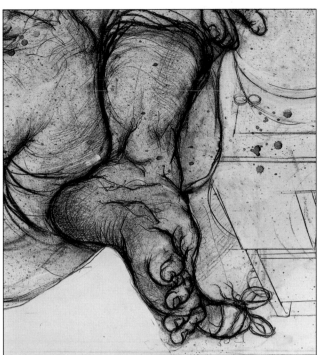

ABOVE These drawings show how important the expression of the feet can be in a drawing.

BELOW Conte drawing of the foot and ankle.

ABOVE This twisted foot shows the construction of the heel and ankle very well. Students frequently underestimate the size of the heel when drawing the foot.

BELOW The hinge joint of the ankle with the large end of the tibia is clearly drawn.

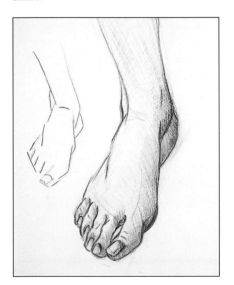

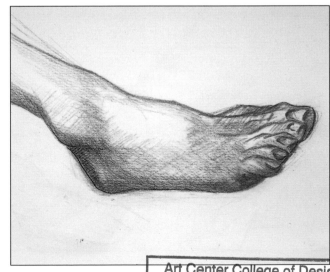

14

CONTEXT AND COMPOSITION

A beautiful drawing of the nude, without any embellishment or development, can be a work of art in its own right. However, there may come a point when we wish to express more by putting the figure into a composition or context.

It is difficult to imagine how profoundly the composition of a picture affects its subject. When we focus our attention on an individual, we are scarcely aware of the other information that our eyes and mind are recording and assessing in the general scene. It is rather like subliminal advertising. The message is slipped in without our being aware of it. A girl seen traveling in the hard light and squalor of a subway train would not immediately be recognized as the same person if she were seen the next day on a park bench in the warm afternoon light.

I think sometimes that students feel I am about to inflict another torture on them when I ask what is meant by putting a figure in context.

The word context comes from the Latin *contextere*, to weave or join together. In the literary sense, the word is applied to those parts of a discourse that precede or follow a passage or sentence, or that are so intimately associated with it that they throw light upon its meaning.

When we put a figure in context, we are putting into the drawing different elements that will enhance and throw light upon the meaning of the drawing. In a sense, we are weaving a story about the person. This is not the same as composition, although composition comes into it.

Looking at the work of good photographers can be a help, for they develop a keen eye for composition and context. Light can play an important part in a composition – a dark, heavy atmosphere will say something quite different from a sunlit room, while a figure beside a small lamp will give a different signal to the viewer. A vast, open studio has a different feel from a claustrophobic room. The type of furnishings or lack of them will say something else. Before you begin a drawing, decide what you want to say in it – think of the "storyline" – then you can begin to choose the type of lighting that would be suitable. If you cannot

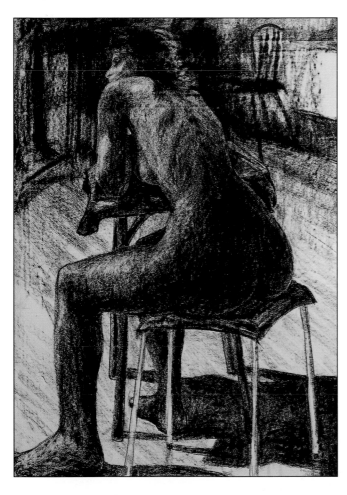

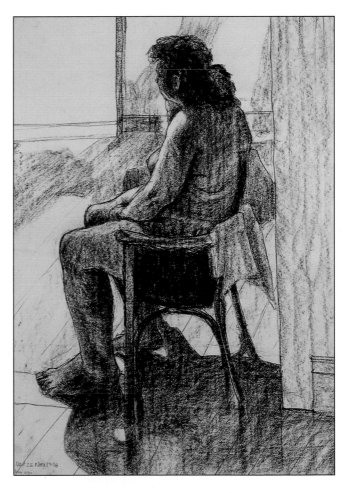

A B O V E In this drawing the heavy shadow pattern made by the chair makes a jagged, hard-edged shape, and this dark tone is carried up into the figure. The strong diagonal thrust of the back leads us to the angle of the shoulder. A small chair has been placed at the far end of the room to create a long linear plane. The atmosphere of the whole piece is charged with energy.

A B O V E In this drawing of the same model again, the charcoal is used roughly on the side, but this time with a gentle touch. Now the light softly bathes the form, there is more space, and the figure is not aggressively in the foreground. The cast shadow on the floor is rounded, and the chair and the full figure gently repeat the motif. As with most compositions based on curves, a calm tranquillity prevails.

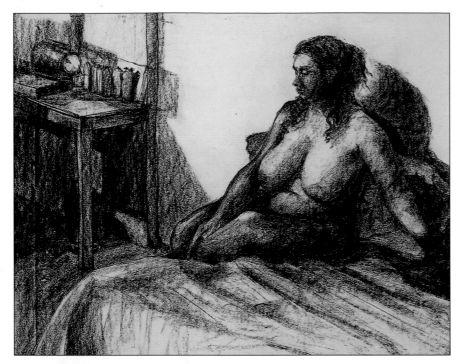

ABOVE This is more than a charcoal drawing of a nude seated on a bed. The harsh light casts a shadow on the wall and obscures part of the figure. The small dresser and unmade bed add to the gloom and suggest a run-down furnished room. The charcoal has been used on the side and not blended, adding a coarse texture that reinforces the message and puts the figure in context.

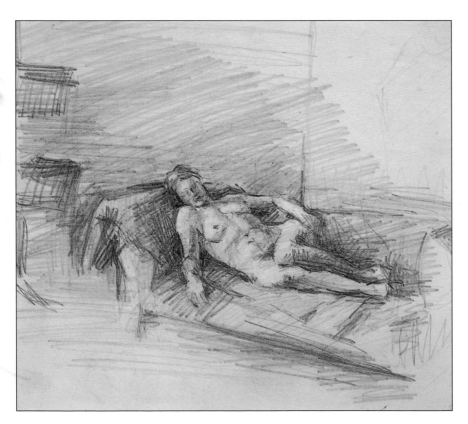

ABOVE A pencil sketch in which the fine and sensitive lines of the pencil are used in layers to create depth and space. By carefully working the darkness around the figure, a minimum of modeling was needed on the figure itself, with the result that the body seems to radiate light.

change the existing light in the studio or room, you can invent a different type of light for the drawing.

Although it is easier and better if you have the opportunity to draw from life, that is not always possible. If you have a life drawing from a class, you can build a room around it. For example, I needed a composition with a nude for my last book. I lightly drew a corner of my living room with a sofa. Then I copied an old drawing of a nude onto the sofa. When I had everything in place – window, curtains, sofa, and figure – I used heavy modeling to throw the room into shadow, with the light coming in through a window. Then my cat came in and sat down in front of the sofa, so I added her to the composition. It was rather like a collage of elements that I assembled in my head and drew.

While context is always a part of a composition, a composition may not put the figure in context. Some compositions are pure divisions of space, made of tone color or decorative pattern, and with little or no content in themselves. Most drawings live in the twilight zone between the two, the basic composition being of paramount importance, although there are some contextual elements in it. The golden rule seems to be that context is optional, but a good composition mandatory.

Composition is the arrangement of shapes that are composed of color, tone, line, or texture. The paper you are working on is a shape, and that shape is an important part of the whole composition. Drawing is like cutting a sheet of paper with scissors, dividing the basic shape of the paper into something that has a certain dynamic energy and interest.

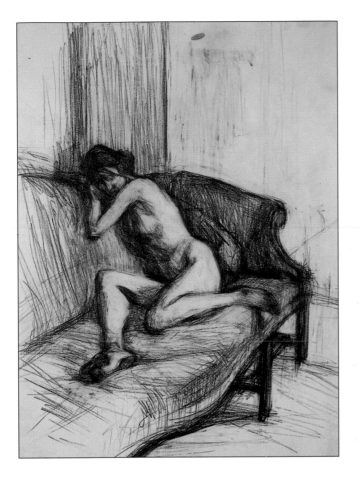

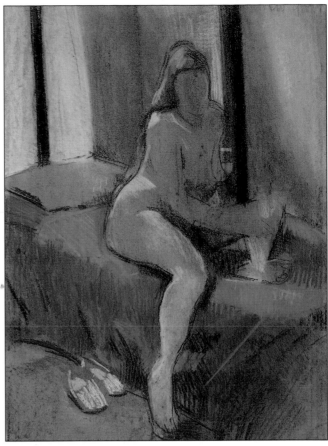

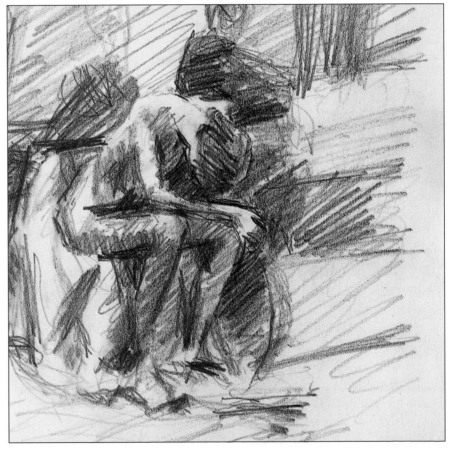

ABOVE The composition of this soft pencil drawing shows how effectively angle can be used against curve. The sensuous lines of the couch lead the eye in, but the model's pose consists of triangles, which provide a tension and strong diagonal thrust across the page.

ABOVE RIGHT A pastel on beige paper in which the artist has silhouetted the figure by drawing the objects in the space around her. The flesh tone of the figure is basically the beige paper showing through, with a few highlights and details drawn in.

RIGHT A pencil sketch in which the artist has defined the shape of the figure and the composition with a few hatching lines. It is a quick note of the composition.

A fascinating drawing in which the rules have been reversed. The drapery, which would normally be roughly indicated, has been drawn with luxurious modeling, and the volume of the old torn cloth carefully observed. The figure, on the other hand, has been drawn very simply against the architectural background of the room.

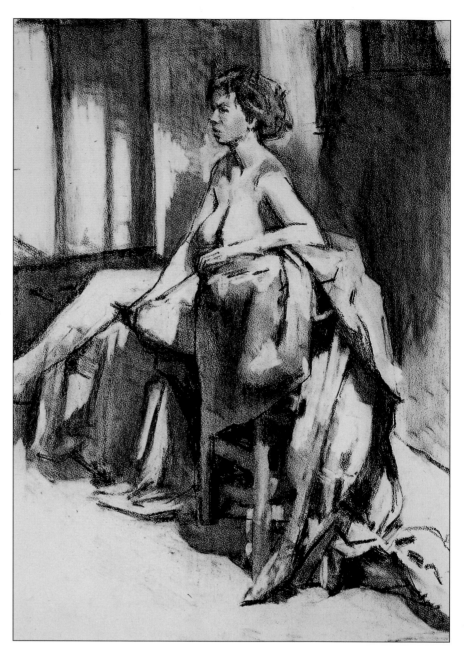

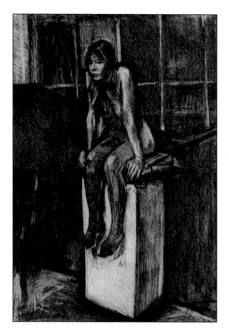

ABOVE Charcoal drawing. This strong composition is based on a grid formed by the windows behind the model and the plinth on which she is sitting. If the model were sitting up straight, the composition would be static, but the forward thrust of her body creates a diagonal line that is carried on in the dark piece of furniture on her left. The contrast in tones make a powerful drawing.

A successful, lively composition demands the careful balancing of all the elements, although the elements or shapes must not be too static or the composition will be boring. There are two types of symmetry in design. Static symmetry is when the sizes of the shapes are equally divisible – in proportion to the numbers 2–4–6, for example. Dynamic symmetry occurs when the shapes are never equal or evenly divisible, but are in proportion to the numbers 3–5–8, for example.

Random forms and scale are the rule in nature, and the more variety you introduce in the shapes you use, the more interesting the composition will become. Remember that the relationship of the sizes is all-important.

Compositions also need a center of interest, but this is seldom placed right in the middle of the work. Instead, it is almost always off-centered to create movement and tension. Of course, there is always a danger of going too far, which is

what makes composition a "balancing act."

Good composition can make an extremely dull subject vitally interesting, while a successful drawing in context will leave the viewer thinking about the person in the drawing, and not just about a figure in a composition. Some of the drawings in this section are drawings in context, and others merge into pure composition. It is interesting to see the difference.

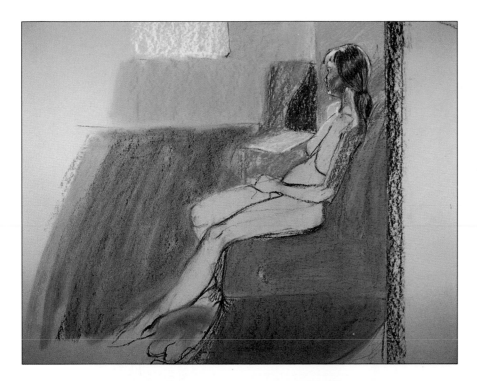

L E F T Soft and hard pastel on tinted paper. The basic forms are laid in with the flat of the pastel to lay out the composition. The background of the room has been invented. A studio spotlight was the actual source of light. The window was added to balance the composition.

B E L O W The finished drawing. Soft pastel has been overlaid with hard pastel hatching lines, and the detail drawn in with a sharp edge of the medium to provide a context for the reflective mood of the model.

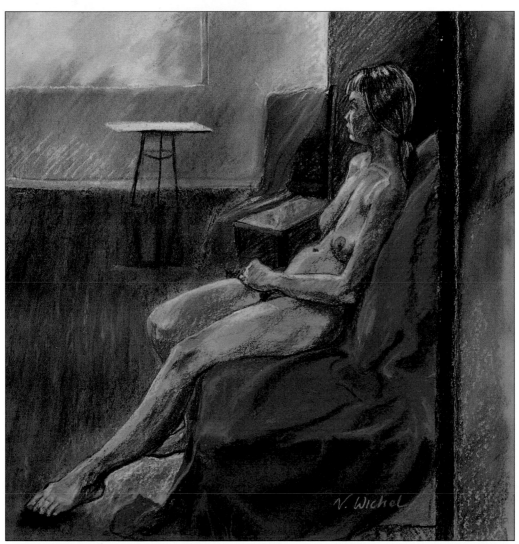

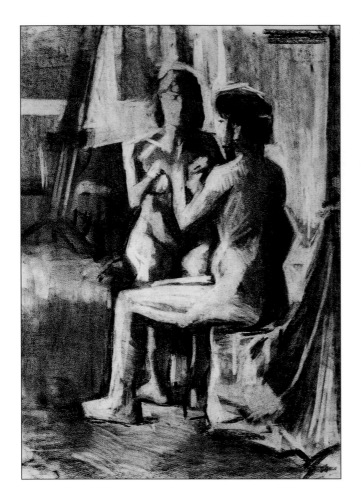

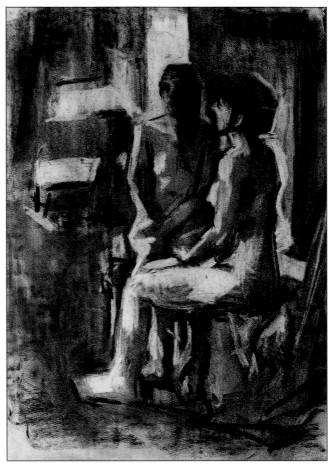

COMPOSING WITH TWO FIGURES

In addition to working directly from the posed figure, the sculptor Auguste Rodin (1840–1917) used to have his models casually walk around his vast studio in Paris. He would observe the natural way they moved, and the relationship and composition of the poses they took while they chatted with one another. It is possible to recapture that atmosphere with all its advantages by working with two models. I have found the self-consciousness and unnatural sterility of an isolated model gives way to a more relaxed atmosphere. Obviously, the emotional content is different, and the contrast between the two figures makes you aware of the individuality of each body. Most important, from the compositional viewpoint, two models offer greater scope.

ABOVE LEFT AND RIGHT Although the models are in the same pose, the mood of these two charcoal drawings is different. It is interesting to see how this difference is produced. In the first drawing the artist has used the zigzag angles of the arms to give a tension and connection between the women. He has repeated the sharp angles in the leg and the easel in the background. In the second drawing there is an introverted and pensive mood. The arms are dropped, and a shadow divides the two women. The sharpness is modified, and quiet curves are used for the arms, back, and thighs. There is also a slight darkening of the light in the room to add to the gloom.

OPPOSITE There is a slightly surrealistic feeling given by the drawing of the male nude behind the model and the aberrant juxtaposition of the flowers. This pastel sketch on tinted paper was drawn quickly and has retained an immediate and fresh quality.

One of the advantages of working with two models is the opportunity to create a greater sense of depth in the picture by placing one model in the foreground and the other at a distance. You will also be able to observe and contrast the different ways in which each model moves and poses, so that the drawing will truly be of two people, not just two figures. Alternatively, you might want to try treating the models as if they were part of an abstract composition. Use the angles in the figures against the curves, emphasizing the decorative pattern of the two bodies in the composition.

One word of caution: always inform your models that they will be posing with someone else; many people object to working with another model.

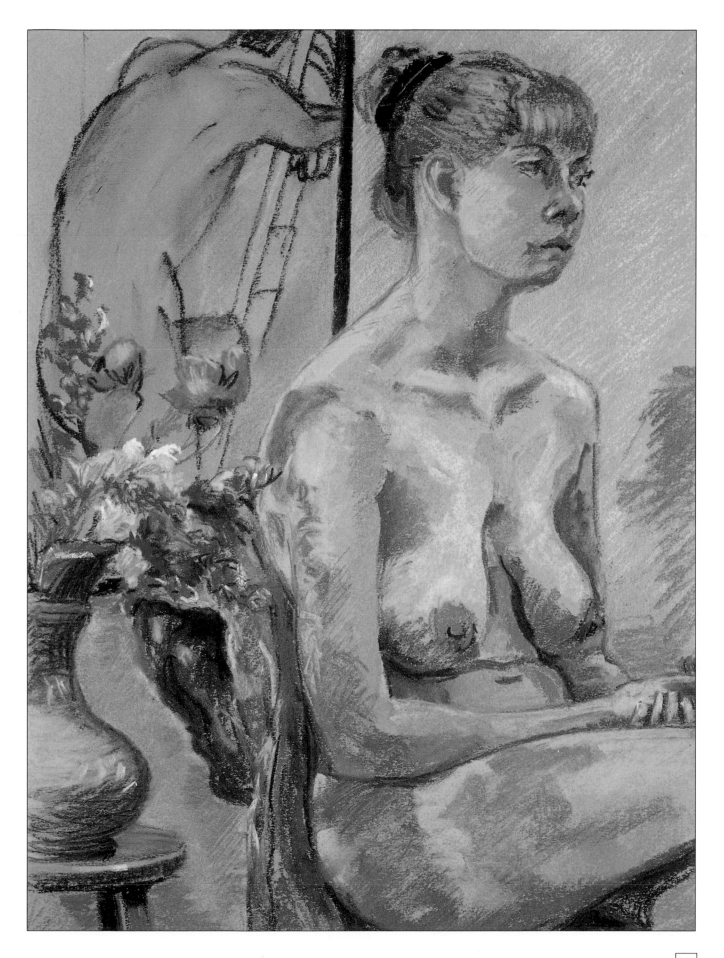

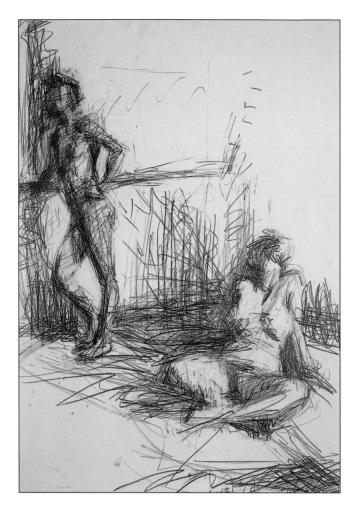

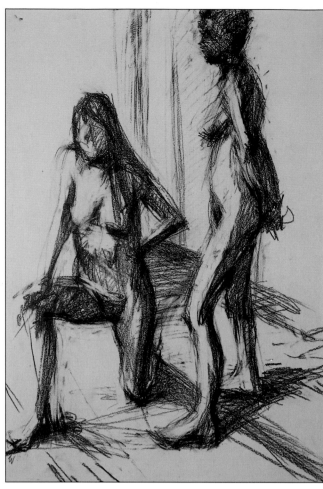

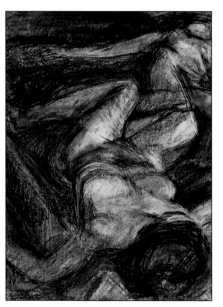

ABOVE The artist has drawn an interesting study in mood and relatedness in this understated pencil sketch. Placing one figure in the foreground gives the composition depth and separates the figures. As the woman in the foreground looks back at the other, our eyes are drawn along the same line of vision to the lone figure looking out of the picture. A question seems to hang in the air.

ABOVE Soft pencil sketch. The figures are arranged as a pattern of contrasting angles and curves. The shadows cast on the floor define the space in the room, while the direction of the light is indicated by the use of shadow and modeling on the figures.

ABOVE This unusual charcoal drawing uses the figures to create an abstract design by posing the models in mirror images of each other. Both charcoal pencils and charcoal sticks were used, and the highlights were brought out with kneaded eraser.

15

USING GOUACHE, WATERCOLOR, AND INK

It has been said that "some artists are born with a brush in their hand and some with a stick." Although most students use several types of media, there is an innate tendency to excel with either the dry stick – charcoal, pastel, conte, and so on – or the brush. This may not be generally apparent at first, but the preference will slowly become obvious.

This section is directed particularly at students who were "born with a brush in their hand."

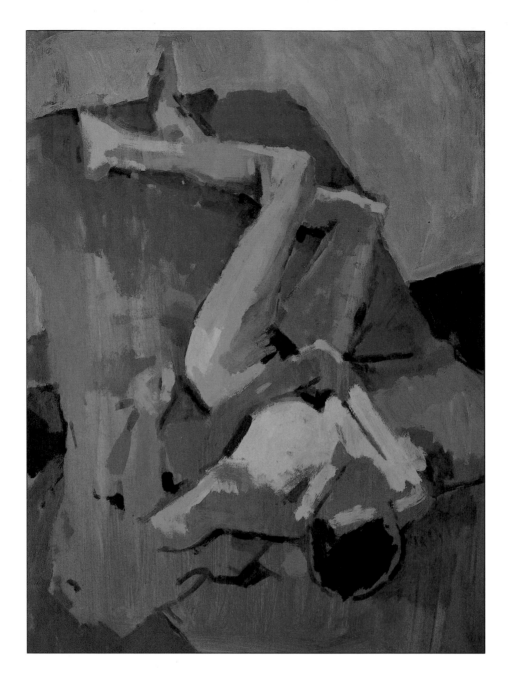

GOUACHE

Gouache is a perfect medium. Use it for itself or as a bridge into life painting with oils, where your studies of tone and modeling will be vital. The structures of all types of painting are established by the shades of the colors. In simple terms, this is setting a light color against a dark one, or dark against light. There are, of course, hundreds of in-between shades that are used in painting. If the model is very fair and is posing against a medium or

dark shade, you can simply paint what you see. A studio, however, may have a white wall, and you will then want to modify the tone sufficiently so that it will contrast with the figure. Changing the color of the wall, but keeping it the same tone, will not have as much effect as changing the shade. If you develop the habit of thinking about the shade first and color second, it will be a great help in your work.

Gouache is composed of artists' pigment and gesso (chalk) with a

ABOVE **The opaqueness of the gouache on strong-colored paper allowed the artist to work here on orange paper. The light pattern on the figure was painted first with a thick flesh tone. This was modified with a light gray in the shadows. The same gray was used in the background. A darker shade of the same gray was put in the foreground under the figure and cloth to stabilize and give weight to the bottom of the composition. The color of the orange cloth is just the paper showing through, with deeper shades of orange gouache in the shadows. The paint has been put on loosely to allow the background color to show through and unite the composition.**

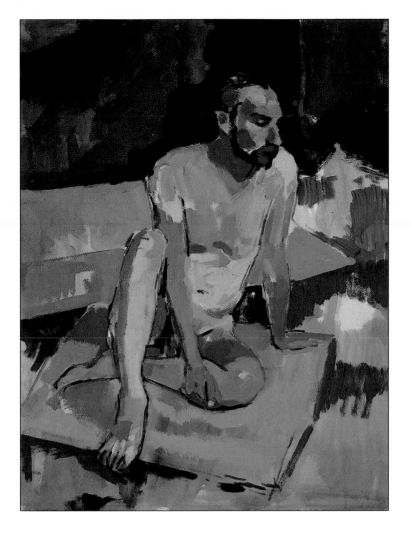

LEFT Gouache on tan paper. The figure has been painted with many shades of the earth colors, sienna and umber. The artist's interest is in the relationship of the various shapes formed by the light, and the composition of figure and background is conceived as an abstract pattern. The black tone behind the head and shoulders off-centers the composition and makes it more dynamic.

weak solution of gum to bind it. Watercolor, on the other hand, is made entirely of very finely ground artists' pigment and a weak solution of gum arabic. It is important to grasp the difference between the two types of paint at the outset. The addition of gesso makes gouache opaque and gives the paint weight. Gouache is frequently added to watercolor if a greater density of paint is needed. Because gouache is a water-based paint, it dries quickly, enabling you to layer one color on top of another. Remember that the underlayer must be completely dry before you apply the next to keep it from mixing with the new paint, which is put on thickly, with very little water. If you wish, part of the underlayer can be left showing through to give a textured, "tapestry" effect. You can, of course, work wet into wet; the paints will blend together well on the paper. Unlike watercolor, which gives a fine, transparent wash when mixed with plenty of water, too much water with gouache gives a nasty and uneven result. Always respect what gouache can and cannot do; if you want a light wash, for example, move to watercolor.

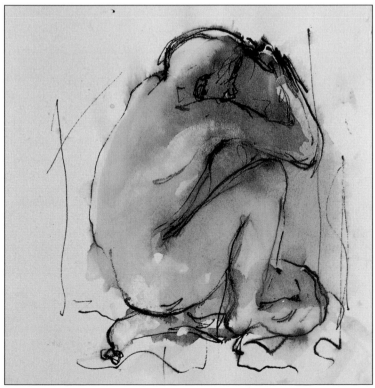

LEFT Here the gouache has been diluted and is used as a semi-transparent wash over an ink drawing, producing a feeling of depth and light quickly.

WATERCOLOR

Watercolor is applied in transparent washes, and the thinner the paint, the more the white paper will shine through and make the color lighter. You should use a good-quality paper so that the color does not sink into the paper, but stays on its surface. Generally with watercolor you should work from light to dark. Apply the light shades first, and gradually the deeper shadows and other tones, so that you slowly build up the drawing. Areas can be lightened by "lifting out" the color with a small piece of natural sponge.

You can work on dry paper, or you can wet part or all of the paper with clear water before you begin. If you are working on a loose sheet of watercolor paper, you should stretch the paper before use to keep it from buckling. This is done by soaking the paper in clear water for a few minutes until it is completely saturated. Allow the extra water to run off and then place it on a board. Fasten the edges of the paper down with brown paper tape to hold it flat as you work. When you have finished, allow the paper to dry completely before cutting it off the board with a mat knife.

BELOW The differences between watercolor and gouache are apparent in this watercolor drawing. The artist has built up layer upon layer of light, transparent washes of color. The soft, blended edges of the blue shadows on the figure tell us that they were put onto a wet flesh tone.

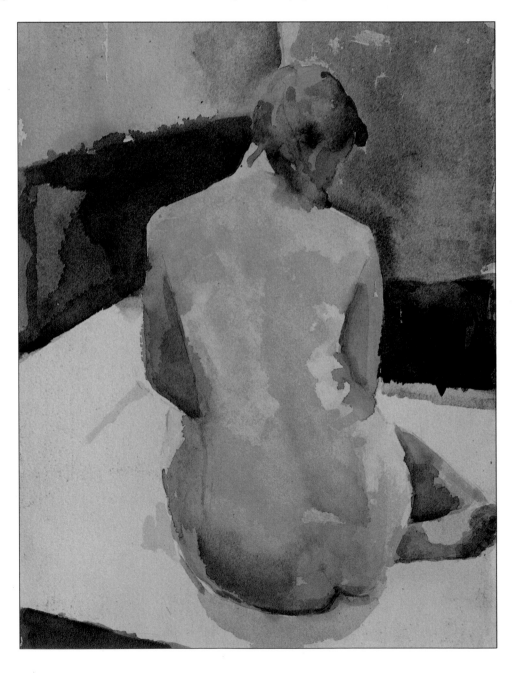

BRUSH AND INK

Use either a sable or a cheaper Chinese brush for brush drawings; you will find that they give very different types of line. The sable has such great resilience that a line can change from fine to thick and back again. The Chinese brush will not "snap back" in the same way, and you have to dip it frequently to repoint it. Nevertheless, it gives a very characterful line with angular movements and abrupt marks. The Chinese brush should be held so that it is almost vertical to the paper.

There is no need to use black ink exclusively. Sepia and sienna are very suitable warm shades for a figure study.

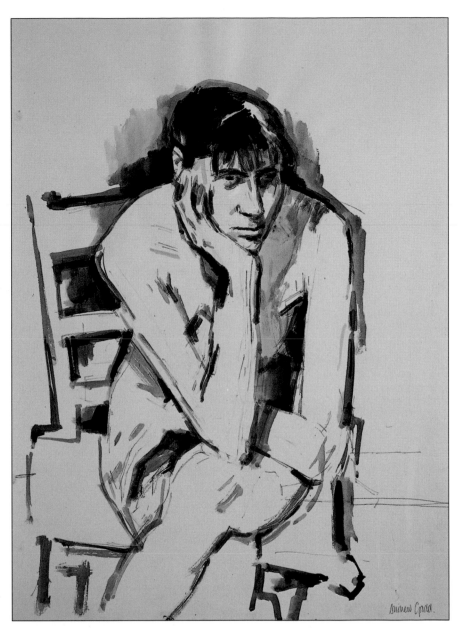

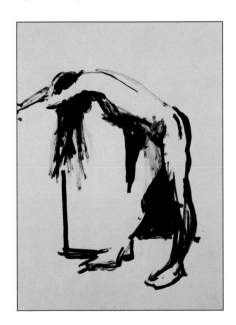

ABOVE AND ABOVE RIGHT These brush and ink drawings were done quickly with the brush following the movements of the figures. No preliminary drawing was made.

RIGHT AND FAR RIGHT How to hold and use a brush and ink. A variety of thicknesses of stroke can be created with this medium.

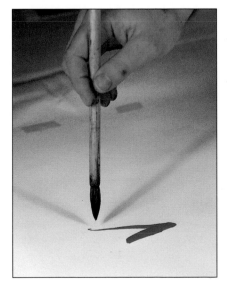

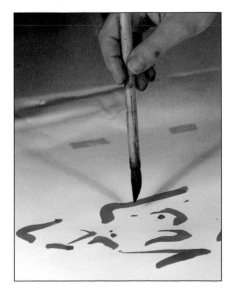

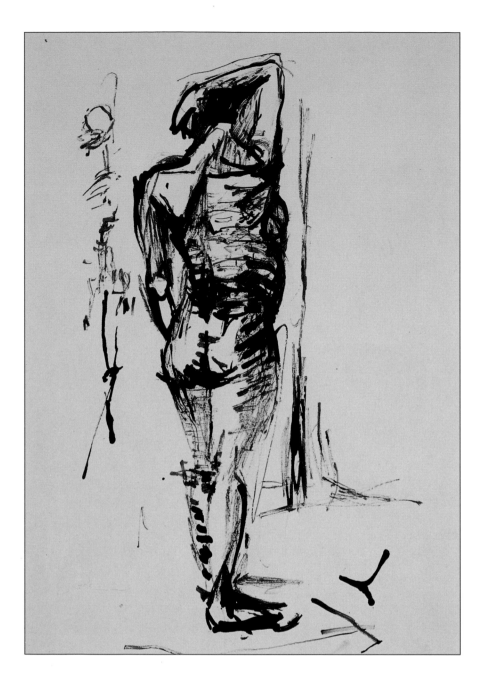

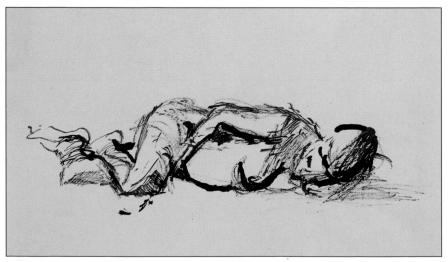

16

CHECKING YOUR
WORK AND IMPROVING IT

Artists use many methods to analyze their work and thus assist in its development.

First and most important is to learn how to diagnose mistakes. You can tear up a work that you feel to be flawed, but unless you understand the mistake, it will not be destroyed with the paper but will be repeated in subsequent work.

How do we know what is wrong? Sometimes the mistake or mistakes are quite obvious; at other times less so. You sense that a drawing does not work and have a vague feeling of unease with it, but cannot quite define what is amiss. It is always useful to use a checklist of common problems, and here are a few ideas to help you analyze your work.

CHECKING THE PROPORTIONS

An error in the proportions of a figure is by far the easiest mistake to see and correct. Use the head as the measure for the figure. As we have seen (pages 23–4), the average person stands between six and a half and seven and a half heads high, although this measurement is frequently exaggerated for certain effects. Michelangelo's figures were 10 or 12 heads tall, for example, and we certainly wouldn't call them mistakes. The width of the body can be checked as well. If it is a standing pose, measure the triangle between the shoulders and the pubic area and across the hips, which will give you the characteristics of the individual's shape.

CHECKING THE BALANCE

Check the balance of the figure by drawing a line down from the balance point (see pages 35–6). On the front of the figure, this is the point between the collar bones. Observe the pose: is the point between the clavicles (the balance point) above the foot or feet on which the weight of the body is falling? If the balance line falls beyond the feet, the figure would not be able to stand. If the figure is standing, check to see that the hips and shoulders are at the proper angles for the weight. The hip over the weight-bearing leg will be pushed up as it bears the weight of the body, while the shoulder over that hip will drop down slightly to counterbalance the figure. If the weight is on two legs, the hips and shoulders will be straight.

If the proportions and balance of the figure are correct but you sense something is still wrong, try these further checks.

CHECKING THE COMPOSITION

When you have been working on a drawing for a period of time, your eyes get accustomed to it and it becomes difficult to see any mistakes. In order to see it with fresh eyes, reverse the image by holding it up to a mirror. The mistake should jump out at you. If it does not, it probably means that the trouble is not in the drawing itself, but in the composition.

By turning the drawing upside down, you will be able to look at the whole of the composition more objectively. Try placing the drawing on a wall with masking tape or standing it across the room so that you can get well back from it.

Frequently, the weight of the composition is not well placed. Some of the lines may be too weak and break up, while other parts may be too heavy and make the drawing one-sided. When you stand back from the drawing, try half-closing your eyes so that you see only the essentials. You want to make sure the drawing is working as a whole.

CORRECTING THE MISTAKES

Few people realize that the best eraser for charcoal or pastel can be found in the kitchen – fresh bread has been the traditional material for erasure for centuries. The slight moisture in the bread lifts off the charcoal, conte, or pastel without rubbing it into the surface of the paper. I have been able to erase very deep colors by this method without damaging the paper. Sharp pencil lines may need a stronger eraser, but try bread first.

Depending on the color of your paper, corrections to ink can be made by whiting out with heavy white or tinted gouache.

DEVELOPING YOUR WORK

At some time or another, we all get the feeling that we are making no progress and that our work is not moving forwards. Worst of all, we may be bored with it. My own solution is to try a radical change of medium. If you have been using charcoal or conte or any of the dry media, change to brush and wash or vice versa. I change to a medium I dislike and one that I do not feel at home with. This forces me to think in a different way about new problems and to leave behind old habits.

If you think your work is too diffident or detailed, try using a large brush – you can try using an ordinary house painting brush, one at least 1 inch (2.5 cm) wide. Use it with poster color on very cheap paper. You are not doing pieces that you will wish to keep; these are loosening-up exercises.

Finally, I frequently put my students' work in a photocopier and adjust the density of the printing to show them what their drawings would be like if they dared to draw with a heavier line.

CHANGING AN UNSATISFACTORY DRAWING

D I A N A   C O N S T A N C E

"If you are going to decide to become a painter, you have got to decide that
you are not going to be afraid of making a fool of yourself." (Francis Bacon).
Rotten drawings are frequently less upsetting to professional painters than to the
amateur. They are considered as one of the risks of the job.

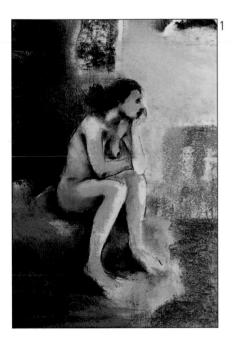

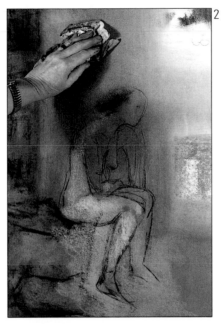

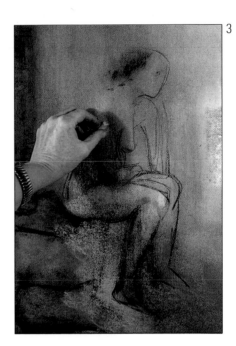

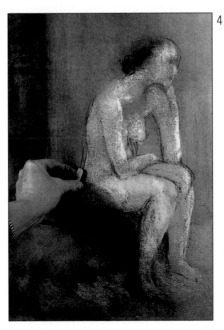

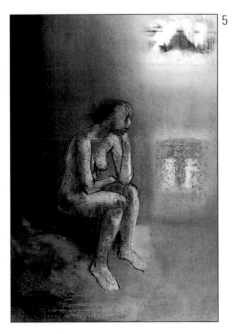

1 The original drawing was wooden and lifeless, and the tones were completely disconnected.

2 The artist is erasing the drawing with a piece of tissue.

3 Here the artist is beginning to redraw.

4 The light tones have been added.

5 The composition has been simplified with the light source established at the fire.

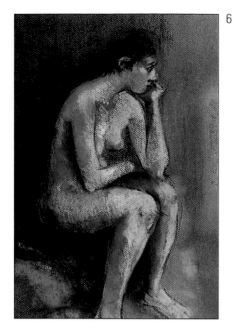

6 The figure has been completely refined, with much more emphasis on the modeling.

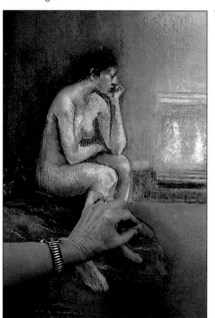

7 A light tone is being added to the drapery, and the light coming from the fire has been emphasized.

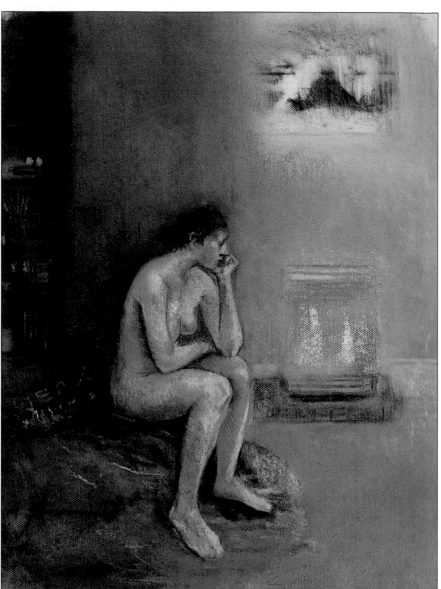

8 The completed drawing bears little resemblance to the original. The center of interest and light source are clearly established with the negative space in the composition now framing the model instead of distracting attention from her, as it was in the original.

17

FRAMING, MOUNTING, AND SHOWING YOUR WORK

Drawings are not the stepchildren of paintings; they are works of art in their own right. Unfortunately, many a good drawing has been ruined by improper treatment or care. The dry-stick media like charcoal, conte, and pastel have to be treated with the greatest respect. The slightest smudging can destroy the crisp effect and make the work quite dead and unsaleable. It only takes a few minutes to fix and cover the work properly.

The caring actually starts before you begin to draw, with the selection of paper. Cheap paper is useful in the beginning when you want to be as free as possible to experiment without worrying about the cost of paper. As you improve, however, you will want the drawing to be permanent. This means avoiding papers made with wood pulp – that is, newsprint, construction paper, lining paper, or brown wrapping paper. If a paper is not acid-free, it will eventually yellow or turn brown.

Many felt-tip pens are made with fugitive inks, which fade very quickly and colored tissue paper is not suitable for collage for the same reason. Charcoal, conte, and pastel are all permanent, but they should be sprayed with a good-quality fixative. Many artists dislike fixing pastel because the light colors are slightly "pushed back" by the damp spray. I prefer to use a light fixative to protect both drawing and the mat board. When a framed pastel drawing is moved, the pastel dust can drift down onto, and soil the bottom of, the mat board. This is particularly galling when work has been sent for exhibition. I always use a good-quality artists' fixative. I have doubts about the long-term effect of using cheap hairspray.

STORING YOUR WORK

Drawings in charcoal, conte, and pastels should be covered with either light tracing paper or with tissue paper. I prefer to use tracing paper, which lies flat and does not pick up the medium. Try to avoid rolling your work. Whenever possible, keep it flat in a drawer or in a portfolio.

MOUNTING YOUR WORK

There are two reasons for mounting your work. First, if it is framed, the paper must be kept away from the glass to avoid condensation marks forming on the drawing. Second, mounting will help to protect your work. A window mat is not only an attractive and professional way to present your work, but it will also keep the work in excellent condition.

You may choose to have your drawing professionally mounted, but if you do it yourself all you need is a mat knife and a steel ruler. If you plan to do quite a lot of mounting, you may want to consider investing in a bevel-edged ruler with a rubber base to stop it from slipping, which makes the job safer and easier. Be sure to change the blade in the knife frequently to keep it cutting cleanly. Use masking tape to anchor the mat board to a table that you have protected with cardboard. If you want a window mat, cut two boards the same size. The first will be used for the window mat, the other for the back board. On the first board, cut out a shape that is slightly smaller than your drawing. Position the window board over the back board. Slide the drawing between the two, taking care not to smudge it, and move it into position so that it is framed by the window. Hold the drawing in place with small pieces of masking tape. The two boards are attached at the top with a tape hinge so that they can be opened to gain access to the drawing.

Whatever type of mat you use, remember to use an acid-free board if you want it to remain white and not leave a ring around your drawing.

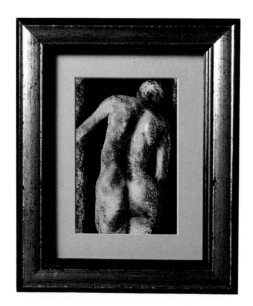

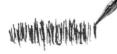

CUTTING A MAT FOR YOUR WORK

D I A N A   C O N S T A N C E

As a student, one of the first things I was taught was how to cut a mat and to present my work properly. Although I objected at the time to this additional work, I quickly learned the value of the professional discipline.

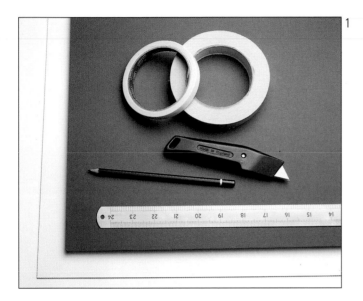

1 These are the basic tools you will need. The mat board, mat knife, steel ruler, masking tape, and double-sided tape.

2 Measure and draw the lines for the window mat.

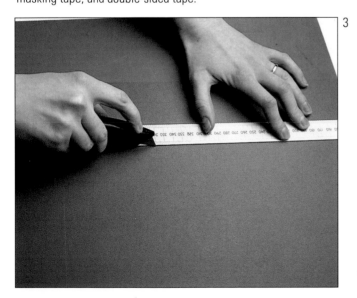

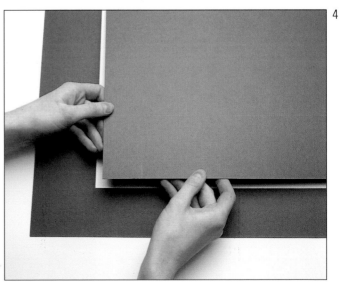

3 Cut window mat. This type of ruler is adequate, but heavier steel rulers with rubber bases are safer.

4 Lift out the cutout from the window board. Save this piece of board; it may serve for a smaller drawing.

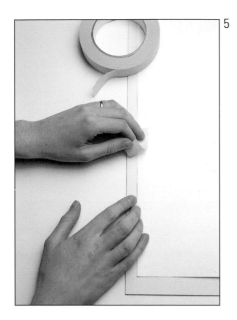

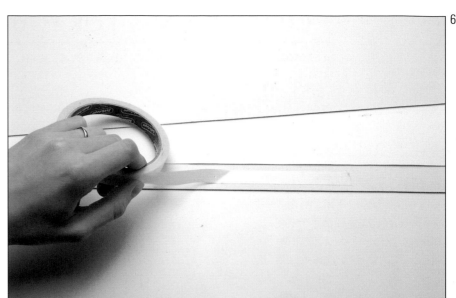

5 Tape the drawing in position on the window mat. If the drawing is a pastel or other delicate, easily smudged media, it should be laid face-down on tracing paper to keep it from smudging.

6 Attach the back board to the window mat with double-sided tape.

7 The finished drawing in its mat. Tracing paper can be put over this if it is to be stored away.

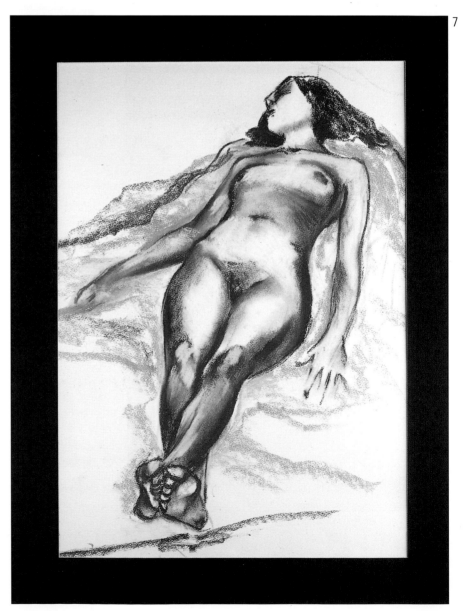

PHOTOGRAPHING YOUR WORK

Before you put your drawing behind glass, you may wish to photograph it. If you plan to submit work for schools or for exhibitions, it is wise to adopt the habit of taking slides and other photographs before framing, because once the glass is in position, the reflections will make photography difficult. If you can work outdoors in daylight, the task will be straightforward. For indoor photography, the best method is to use a tripod and two photographic flood-lamps with film that is color-corrected for tungsten light. Flash can also be used, but experimentation is essential. If you stand too close, the work will be bleached out; if you are too far away, the white paper will look murky.

FRAMING YOUR WORK

There are two schools of thought about framing. One is that permanent framing is for something you want to keep; the other is that a frame is merely a temporary home for a drawing that is just a passing guest until it is sold or replaced.

Most professional artists and many students prefer temporary frames or exhibition frames. These are usually made of wood so that they can be sanded down and repaired to remove the damage that frequently occurs when you send work to an exhibition. I have several standard-size frames that accommodate the different sizes of paper I work on, and I can change an old drawing for a new one in 20 minutes. I clean the glass with denatured alcohol, secure the back board with cut brads, and put brown paper tape over the seam between board and frame to keep the dust out. The new work is ready to go.

Remember that clip frames are not usually acceptable for mixed exhibitions. The glass frequently breaks or comes loose, and the organizers refuse to handle them for safety reasons.

Artists' magazines give advance notice of all forthcoming exhibitions.

Picture Credits

INDEX

Page numbers in *italics* refer to illustration captions.

A

aging, changes to body 21, 25
arms, anatomy of 17, *19*, 20

B

balance, line of 33–9
   checking 120
   contrapposte 33, 36
balance points 35–8
   in movement 42
Botticelli, Sandro 7
bounced light 56, 60
Brunelleschi, Filippo 47
brushes 13
   Chinese 13, 117
   nylon 13
   sable 13, 117
   squirrel 13

C

charcoal 11
   erasing 11
   modeling with 66–9
   sticks 66
   suitable paper for 11, 66
   using with pastels 86, 90–1
composition 104–12
   checking 120
   composing with two figures 110–12
conte 12, 62
context 104–6
contour drawing 31–2
contrapposto, see balance
co-ordination, hand to eye 30–2
correcting and improving work 119–22
Cranach, Lucas 99
crosshatching 71–5
   with two colors 72–3

D

David, Jacques 7
Degas, Edgar 7, 82
Woman in a Tub 9
Delacroix, Eugène 7
   The Crusaders Entering Constantinople 7
   Death of Sardanapalus, study for *9*
developing your work 120

E

easel, position at 27
emaciated figures 23, *24*
erasers 11, 12, 120
   drawing with 62, 66
eye level, model in relation to 48–9

F

feet, anatomy of 19, *21*, 101
   drawing 101–3
felt-tip pens 13, 79
figure, female and male 21, 23, *24*
fixative 14, 124
foreshortening 49–54
   diagrammatic sketch for 50
framing drawings 127

G

gouache 114–15
graph paper, use of 27
graphite sticks 11
ground plane 48

H

hands, anatomy of 17–18, 98
   drawing 97–100
   movement 100
head, drawing 92–6
   foreshortened 96
   proportions of 25

I

ink 117–18

K

Kitaj, R. B. 83
Klee, Paul 79

L

legs, anatomy of 18–19, *20*, 21
light 55–75
   expressed through line 62–4
   expressed through modeling 57–61
   types of 56–7
line drawing 76–81
   beginning 79
   drawing materials 79
   roundness, creating 78

M

Manet, Edouard 7
   Dejeuner sur l'herbe 7
measurement 26–8
   for foreshortening 49
Michelangelo
   Adam, study 7
modeling, compared with line drawing 58–9
   with charcoal 66–9
   with pastels 58–61
   with pencil 70–1
movable grid measuring system 27
movement 40–5
muscles 19–21
mounting drawings 124–6

N

negative space, drawing 28–9, 49

P

paper, types of 14
   for charcoal 11, 66
   for line drawing 79
   for pastels 83
pastels
   blending 86
   erasing 83
   hard pastel 87
   layering 90
   line drawing with 79
   modeling with 58–61
   suitable paper for 83
   types 12–13
   using two shades 88–9
   using with charcoal 86, 90–1
pencils 11
   colored *11*
   line drawing with 79
   modeling with 70–1
pens, bamboo 13, 18, 79
perspective 47–54
   in line drawing 77
photographing drawings 127
planes of the body 647
proportion 22–7
   checking 120
   measurement of 27
protecting and storing work 11, 14, 124

R

Rodin, Auguste 110
Rubens, Peter Paul 7, 36

S

Schiele, Egon 64
self-portraits *94, 95*
shoulders, anatomy of 17, *18*
silverpoint 70
skeleton *16*, 17, 18
skull 25, 93–4
slow motion drawings 43
spine, curvature of 17, 36
spotlight, use of 56, 60
symmetry 108

T

tendons 19
Titian 7
trunk, anatomy of 18
two figures, composing with 110–12

W

watercolor 116

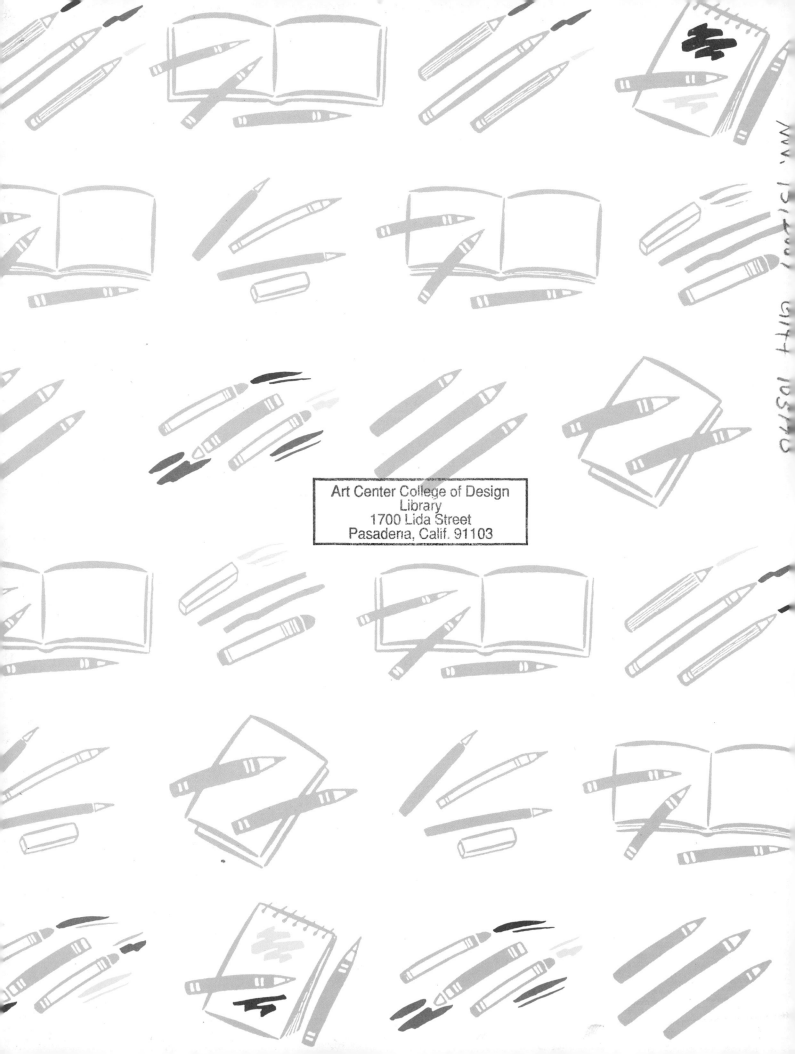